NOTES FROM MADOO

NOTES FROM MADOO

Making a Garden in the Hamptons

ROBERT DASH

A Frances Tenenbaum Book
HOUGHTON MIFFLIN COMPANY
Boston New York
2000

Visit our Web site: www.hmco.com/trade.

Library of Congress Cataloging-in-Publication Data

Dash, Robert.

Notes from Madoo : making a garden in the Hamptons / Robert Dash.

p. cm.

Essays extracted from the author's biweekly gardening columns in the East Hampton star.

"A Frances Tenenbaum book."

ISBN 0-618-01692-9

1. Gardening—New York—Sagaponack. 2. Dash, Robert—Homes and haunts—New York—Sagaponack. 3. Madoo Garden (Sagaponack, N.Y.) I. Title.

SB453.2.N7 D37 2000

635.9'09747'25—dc21 00-020062

Book design by Anne Chalmers

Printed in the United States of America

QUM 10 9 8 7 6 5 4 3 2 1

The material in this book was previously published, in somewhat different form, in the *East Hampton* (New York) *Star*.

For my parents,

Father there, Mother here,

in whose garden Madoo began

CONTENTS

PREFACE

MAY OF 1965 found me in a car with the late realtor Judge Harold Hallock, feeling down and daunted. Nothing at all seemed suitable. But then—

"What is that?"

"Oh, just an old barn. You don't want that. Falling down. It's been on the market for the longest time."

"But I do."

"Do you want to see it?"

"No need. It winked at me."

What I had seen was the roofline of an eighteenth-century hay barn sailing above a hedgerow, in from Main Street, Sagaponack.

"It's on an acre. Some outbuildings, too. All really old. You might get another acre."

A year later, it was mine. In 1967 I moved in and began making the garden I call Madoo.

NOTES FROM MADOO

INTRODUCTION

English Bones, American Flesh

My garden is at the far eastern end of Long Island, in New York State, in a town settled in 1656. It is set amidst fields continually farmed since that time, and one would need a maul to separate it from its profoundly English influences. Yet it might take a wedge struck with equal force to pry it from its continuous involvement with the patterns of abstract expressionism, a largely American form of painting.

Within that pattern much else went toward the making of my garden: a love of Indian paths, rather like the secret walks small children make (which counts a lot for how one moves through my garden); an admiration of the roan beauties of abandoned farmland pierced by red cedars laced and tied by dog roses, honeysuckle, and brown, dry grass; the memory of a meadow of a single species of short, gray-leaved, flat-topped, open-flowered goldenrod, whose October display was feathered by hundreds of monarch butterflies. I have a stubborn Calvinist belief in utility, which causes me to plant vegetables among flowers, use herbs as borders and berry bushes as ornamentals. The brutish littoral climate leads me to choose only such plants as have infinite stamina. There are recollections of an ancestor who planted hollyhocks at the gate and lilacs out back—but all gardens are a form of autobiography. Moreover, as a painter, I am predelicted toward shape, mass, and form and have learned that the predominant color of all gardens is green and all the rest is secondary bedeckment. Finally, there is something else—a fierce addiction to privacy, which is why my windbreak is thicker than it need be.

Madoo, which in an old Scots dialect means "My Dove," is the name of my garden of 1.98 acres, and I have been at it now since 1967. I have gone about it as I would a painting, searching for form rather than prefiguring it, putting it through a process more intuitive than intellectual. The blunders are there to learn from; the successes, more often than not, are the result of bold throws. I started from the house and went out toward the edges, often revising solid achievements until they seemed made of finer matter, like marks and erasures of work on paper, which sometimes may be torn and fitted again in collage.

Although I like white on white (the 'Duchess of Edinburgh' clematis on a white fence over *Rosa* 'Blanc Double de Coubert'), and I like to whiten white by throwing autumn clematis (*C. terniflora*) over yew, 'Huldine' over holly, the major push is for green on green. I have never cared much for all-gray gardens or all-blue gardens; indeed, I am not certain that they are ever successful, color being too quixotic to control in that fashion, full of lurking betrayals, so that sky blue becomes sea blue or slate blue and then not blue at all. The air over my garden, from whose several points I can see the Atlantic surf, is full of a most peculiar double light, rising and falling, and is itself one of the heroes of my landscape, kinder to foliage and bark than to flowers. Wild air will always do the painting. I have increased the atmosphere's multiple shimmer by putting in three small ponds, above whose surfaces small mists sometimes gather. In contrast I have made darkness with a copse of twisted, pruned arctic willows and another of a spinney of fastigiate ginkgoes, the former underplanted with a mix of epimedium, woodruff, Japanese wood anemones, and ferns, and both washed with the littlest of spring bulbs. Paths are of brick, pebbles, or setts, or disks of telephone pole, or grass. Curves alternate with strict, straight geometries, the better to bound, heighten, and confine the predominantly relaxed, semiwild, superabundant atmosphere I like.

A meadow garden has been quite successful. Formerly, it was lawn giving a rather dull view from the dining table, made duller by summer heat and inevitable drought. America is no climate for lawns. I did not starve the soil to make the meadow but plunged robust, thrusty perennials through the grass into pits carefully nourished with well-rotted manure and much peat moss. It is roughly oval with a backing of Nootka cypress, cryptomeria, and rhododendron, whose darks perfectly outline the brighter foil of foliage.

To my way of seeing, a garden is not a succession of small rooms or little effects but one large tableau, whose elements are inextricably linked to the accomplishment of the entire garden, just as in painting all passages conduce to the effect of the whole. Lack of keyed strength in any one of them may lower the pitch and thrust of the finished canvas.

A muting of a too-perfect area is often in order, no matter

how lovely it might be. Just so I have found 'Silver Moon' clematises are too huge a cynosure to be acceptable to the general garden, and I have taken them out. One can very definitely have too much of a good thing, unless it be some grand groundcover like *Lamium* 'Nancy', whose very modest performance excludes it from the egregious. Subtlety is always more alluring. The quieter painting enters the heart and stays, when one of tremendous impact has long since faded away.

I do not paint in the way that I garden or garden as I would employ the brush, although the process is often the same—both are arts of the wrist, the broadest, largest sort of signature, if you will, highly idiosyncratic, the result of much doing, much stumbling, and highly intuited turns and twists before everything fits and adheres to the scale of one's intention. A good tree must often be moved to a more reticent spot when it begins to dominate and thus ruin the total orchestration. Beautiful tunes don't end up as symphonies, nor do witticisms write books. Certain flowers may emblazon a room but be abusive to a fine garden. For that reason and that of stamina and the ability to take the brunt of the climate (I am in Zone 7a, whose average lowest temperature is five to zero degrees Fahrenheit), I choose older varieties of the plant kingdom, whose foliage and blossom are, more often than not, circumspect and discreet.

I am now becoming more geometric. In front of the winter house and winter studio I have just installed a brick path I call a view-swiper. It is 120 feet long (flying out to the potato fields and to the ocean, bringing all that fine view inside the purview of the garden as if it were mine), 8 feet wide at the near end, 6 at the far, with 80 roses ('Fru Dagmar Hastrup') on the sides. The far border will have other, taller rugosa roses and daylilies mixed with teasels. The site is but a narrow spur attached to my property, surrounded by changing crops whose patterns of growth and tilling are overwhelmingly seductive, requiring only the simplest sort of anchor to moor the peninsula.

My canvases now have changed, too, and are rather like foliant form held very close to the eye. Both gestures, then, are new for me, and the feeling from both is a bit scary, akin to that of someone in the middle of a new high-wire act performing over a slowly withdrawing net. The air of gardens and paintings now seems to me to be filled with a wild, deliciously cold oxygen through which I can still see the first plain view of the working barns I converted three decades ago, gray above a blowing field of grass. That verdure, it seems to me, was the very soul of the place "working backwards, year by year," as John Koethe wrote in "The Near Future," until it "reached the center of a landscape."

The English bones with which I began now seem entirely covered by what I have done, but that is the way of flesh.

The Death of a Field

❧

Spiritual equanimity is so finely worked that all wild, wounding, or awesome events fire the brain but briefly. "Take heart," said Aeschylus, "for suffering, when it occurs at its highest, lasts but a little time." Longer, one's whole being might implode. Of the many mercies of spring, one is that we perceive its huge regeneration in a small quantum, as symbol rather than distributed occurrence. A single spear of a daffodil strap blue above yellow straw does nicely for the whole. Or it may be the moment we smell odors again and know that the great uncorking has begun once more.

Just so, the moment when roses are high, June becomes summer. And so the day late in autumn when the sky contracts and seems made of stone and one thinks one sees the diagonal zip of a snowflake cutting across the cedars. A moment as cold as the moment you are no longer loved and it is hard to breathe.

In the open fields of Sagaponack, spring is the first brown throw of earth falling over rye cover as a tractor cuts broadly, Sagg Main Street to Sagg Pond and then, engine regeared, pond back to street. Directly to the south this is, in Foster's fields, the widening brown finally meeting a horizon of sand where brown stops and Atlantic flats begin and skies begin to rise wet once more.

But not in the field to my west, not any year ever again. Ink started wounding it on a first bill of sale in 1968, and then more ink on more bills (three times in one year once), while profits bloomed from the contracts and rolled over in a mulch of lawyers, agents, and speculators. Each year the large question as to whether it would be farmed went up and down Main Street.

And then one winter in the mid-seventies large, bright rented cars rolled through the field, randomly scattering wintering geese. Strangers sat fogging the glass or got out dressed in the most improbable clothes and pointed. Day after day, up and down my drive, the dark blue and the black cars with whitewalls, doors slamming. Agents, brimming with good will, made the most flourishing gestures (rather like sweeps of the cavalier introducing audience to players, singers to orchestra), their gloved hands flashing above the empty winter stubble as if gathering all of the homes and the lands and the gardens of Sagaponack, which too were part of the vibrant tableau offered for sale.

The field was done in. Wooden sticks sprayed Day-Glo orange gored the earth, and red rags and flags were tied to the branches of the hedgerow. Concrete columns called "monuments" were slipped into the outlines of the plats. An eighteenth-century English oast house was disassembled, beams numbered and stacked for shipment to the lot immediately adjoining mine. The profile of any oast house is eerily similar to the stacks of Three Mile Island.

All was surveyed in the bright light of plane geometry, as

was all of America, a much-abused idea from the Age of Enlightenment that has been swallowed whole. Everything had to have a right angle. Everything had to be logical and orderly—which is why the view of the Great Plains is so right from on high and so utterly dismal on the ground. One drives a hundred miles on impeccably straight roads to reach and cross other roads at precise right angles where nothing is, neither name nor house nor tree nor stone.

The road connecting Sagg Main Street with the newly charted Territory of the Field took fifteen feet of my own right of way in order to complete a mandatory fifty-foot width (to accommodate only four houses) and was straight-lined and then made two right-angle turns around my property. The corners were smoothed a bit in pale polite rural amenity. The road was asphalted, mounded for runoff; its abominable cobblestone curbs have drains, and slightly sloped embankments frame it, either side.

And then the trucks came and the cesspools and the leaching pits and the foundations and the underground wires and all the internal driveways on the little plots. One house is so close to Sagg Pond that its cesspool pours nitrogenous effluent into the water. Algae bloom, and the eventual eutrophication of Sagg Pond earnestly has begun. Dead water is, after all, compatible with dead earth.

I built a fence. The road turns directly in front of the glass of my winter studio. Headlights would shine on the walls where I paint. I stripped the lower branches of the two thousand black pines I planted over a period of five days some years ago, cutting down some entirely, to put the timber planks in the middle of the rows, relinquishing a good eight feet of my land in order to have the height I needed. Later I planted privet on both sides of the fence, for the black pines were dying.

I lost my daily walk through the field to the pond and the sight of the steeple of the Bridgehampton Presbyterian church. I can no longer see my first studio across the pond. A house blocks it out. My street address changed, for I was, of course, no longer on a dirt spur off Sagg Main Street but on a macadam road.

Of course, there are the paintings of the field, but I am not interested much in paintings of vanished landscapes, and I loathe nostalgia. What I had to do was cope with the extraordinary sense of dislodgment, the feeling that kilter was gone. A hole as black as any in outer space still rises in my throat when I roam through this vandalism.

Any object of worth has its little history, be it only one of provenance. The history of this field is invisible, although for centuries it had been a marvel of fertility, from Indian to colonist by royal patent, and was farmed by the same family from colonial times to that dreadful May of 1967 when the last of the line went south. The field was tended and cherished like any object of *vertu*. Unlike porcelain, however, whose pieces may be glued, the field is valueless and irreclaimable, the light of centuries of harvest snuffed.

Color, a Point of Hue

Painters manipulate color the way birds know bugs and squirrels, nuts, and how to codify the instinct or teach it is daunting. I am, I know, a fool for writing about it.

But bear with me as I begin my garden in 1967, gardening in earnest on a plot owned, not rented, and with the intention that it will be a sort of lifelong making of garden pictures. Not rooms. I think of exhibitions, not houses. At that time I unscrewed the lid of all the vegetal shapes I could muster in a single season in much the way that an art student might go berserk in an unattended art store.

As I recollect that burgeoning summer of plant terrifics, tithonias roared over *Astilbe* 'Fanal' in tandem with bocconias and dahlias and, I think, gladiolas. Pumpkins and gourds and citron roiled with the moonflowers and morning glories, and asparagus plumed an edge in an attempt to confine it all. I cannot recall what else went in jam, pack, ram, all in a small elled cove made by the studio barn, a hall, and two fixed-up shacks. By midsummer, growth stalled the doors, windows got blocked, friends rolled their eyes. My elderly schnauzer got lost in it all and was located only by her whine. It was a seething microcosm of shape, shadow, and rampancy, and I loved the heft of it all. Green eruption followed green eruption like greenhouses exploding or a whirlwind through silage, and I was in billy-goat bliss.

Over a quarter of a century later, I am perhaps more circumspect. What is here now is a mainly green garden. Foliant umbrage is silvery and cottony below and lanced, blunted, toothed, or indented; strap, ovate, and round; margined with white and yellow or speckled silver. Matte or shiny satisfactions take sun, wind, and wet, beginning ruby or tourmaline in spring and echoing them in autumn. The livery is so grave and complete and calming that I wish I were an herbivore. What is it if not superb glissando, rows of unornamented pewter plate on a dark wooden table or emerald crystals carving the very air? Bloom is an afterthought. Almost an impertinence.

But while this green flood was collecting, it soon became clear to me that this perfect color field would need some framing, and so the garden's inanimates—fences, railings, bowls, posts, arbors, doors, gates, benches, and tools—began to wear high hues of the sort that would make indoor eyeballs wince but were quite suitable outside. Didn't da Vinci say that the air does the painting?

What I have now are great brown Korean export bowls (oil and mustard), Aladdin size, bouqueted with green, and natural bamboo tying stakes and even scarlet surveyor's sticks, echoes of growth (or bloom, if you wish) so necessary to a small garden, where, unless one is a tireless plunger and lifter of annuals, it is impossible to expect unceasing display. Like italics, the geometry of framing is further satisfied by railings painted in matte chartreuse, the color of infantile and autumnal foliage. All through the downs of August it sounds a fine note, and it is insouciant under hoarfrost and snow.

A certain purple I mixed, one much barded with rose and cinder, became soft and hazy, very much like those grays beloved of landscape painters. A double tonality of it went up the gazebo, paled to two evening fogs on the roofs, remaining brusque and unmodified on the Chinese Chippendale railings below. It was Manet who thought that the very color of the air was violet. A stained black octagonal table sits in the center, holding a disk of limestone on which is a blue pitcher and washbasin. There are eight black octagonal stools on the pale floor. The same dark purple went on a section of Carpenter Gothic fencing and on two eleven-foot arches made of plumbers' piping in the center of the potager. That a blue clematis twines on it seems irrelevant, for blooming or not, the arches never fade. The wheelbarrows became not fire engine red but more like drying tangerine skin. Three mirrors on each side of some outlying sheds counterpoint the effect. A curved bedroom door opening to a long path gets painted according to the viridity of the season—yellow in spring, dark blue when leaves adolesce. It takes a coat as orange as the barrows when the ginkgoes go gold. And cream Panama hats sprout jauntily on the odd post and gate, and I have begun collecting lengths of hose in terra cotta. But I miss black. The winter and summer houses and the two studios attached have mintons and mullions of blue with green inserts. I begin to think that black eaves would look fine against the aging cedar shakes. A pale green fence abuts an even paler stile set above woodruff and epidemium. Goldfish circle under the new Chinese bridge, which is to be stained red and yellow on certain of its uprights, and the rest will be allowed to weather unadorned. But I think a shine of wax or oil might do. I path in faded earthen setts and bricks and on one rectangular terrace have placed purple and green boxes on dark wooden feet. In winter they are filled with prunings of red- and yellow-twigged dogwood, and the birds—cardinals, jays, grackles, and mourning doves—assemble on the nearby stone bench washed in chick-cracked corn.

What I do may not be for others. We all practice seduction in unique fashion. Yet my heart leans on green, for it is a world-class color, at once oasis and Eden. We agree, don't we, that the green gardens of the Italian Renaissance are unrivaled, unless by that most nearly perfect garden since . . . Rousham? "Green, green," said Lorca, "I would have you green/green hair/green branches." I take green to be not only the predominant color of a flourishing garden but the emblem of its aspiration, the barometer of its health, the very mirror of its finish. Green is its basic architecture clothed, which then becomes its ever-changing form. Great gardens have been green all through, with grass walks and mossed and vined walls enclosing generous, remarkably clipped yews like a great green house of grand green rooms roofed by the light of the sky. Green is the color that springs to mind when we think of Eden and the color one most anticipates as a garden is approached.

Of the other colors, I confess indifference to all of their seductive frailties. Never do I consciously think in terms of them, for they get in the way of form and are at their epitomes but the charming rewards of fine gardening (rather like those tan cities of northern Italy through which bright lines of washing sail out and then are drawn back in).

White, however, I do think of. White gates and benches and houses which are almost like canvas not yet covered, or the blaze of paper in Cézanne watercolors. A white clematis on an old piece of chipping white fence, pouring over and falling through a white rose. An enormous *soulieana* rose against hedge privet in bloom is a second bit of deliberate engineering I have tried and liked, and that annually works to great satisfaction. And wild daisies are making marvelous stops and explosions throughout the garden and in the fields, glinting like felled clouds or crumbs of our mostly white, monitoring summer skies.

And now that I think of it, I do have another white, having thrown on a native holly I stemmed to a single fat trunk a large-flowered midsummer clematis. (The one over the rose is a double early one and more like old piano keys or linen than white.) This one annually threads through the holly leaves and looks whiter for such dark backing, a carefully considered fountain effect that appears charmingly relaxed and casual to the point of seeming accidental. But the clematis, with its own contribution of lighter green leaves, looks quite splendid bare of bloom, the fountain form being just broad enough and high enough to fit the general elevations of the surrounding plantings. And yes, there is still another white clematis, the autumn C. *paniculata* (now *terniflora*) robing the yew hedge by the summer studio.

White seems to have a way of leading the eye to other whites, which reds and yellows and blues do not, and I have taken a walk around and around the garden and noted how many times and in how many subtly varied hues white appears. Dew will appear white in certain light. We have begun to have night fog. The countryside is mostly white houses in a green landscape with daisies and dog roses in hedgerows and field turns and of course potatoes blossoming, all as complete a large gardened landscape as one would ever wish to design, with pickets, too, and steeples all made whiter by graying shingled sheds and overarching elms and maples. Psychologists, when faced with the visually obsessed, call this alertness to seeing one color and only that color, as if it were everywhere and anything, the phenomenon of "setting."

I proceeded again through the green of my garden to see what whites I could find, their existence rarely one of deliberation but more often based on feeling, such as the one that makes painters put more of what is in the brush on the canvas or composers flutter strings below horns the better to swell the sound.

Last autumn I broke apart two rows of peonies I had in the propagating bed. Half I reserved for a bed beside a curved walk where I was after bushiness, and half I struck at random in the heart of a small meadow garden (which was, in truth, part of the lawn I got tired of mowing).

The peony is *Festiva maxima*, an introduction of 1851, a double, doubling white, sometimes flushed with the pallor of unsunned white flesh, sometimes flecked with clear cadmium red at petal tip, but still as white as big balls of wet pulled cotton. It is entirely successful in its new setting behind tall stems of timothy and milkweed and a clump of white yarrow I don't recall having put in at one end of the little meadow. And then daisies as fine as daisies can be.

So provoking a color is white, I even have brambles I don't mind and dog roses and mushrooms on the lawn, *fraises des bois* in constant bloom, and chamomile. The awns of some grasses in early morning are white, and mock orange, and the old memory of viburnum and the new one of chionanthus. *Clematis recta* is now in bloom, and campion. I have a tiny old carnation raised from Allwood seed, and Japanese roof iris. I had white tulips. The Chinese dogwood is now out. And other things pale pink, pale blue, pale red, and pale yellow that white seems to appropriate as its own.

I have put out a white rocking chair. The paint is old and over blue paint. It shines. Brown and tan and gray pebbles beneath it get washed in the midday sun.

The Chemical-Free Garden

Gardening in the opening years of the new millennium is a concern for how each and every garden conduces to the whole, agreeably echoes preexisting surrounding foliage, aids and abets wildlife flow, the passage of birds and seeds, maintains the purity of groundwater, takes air as it arrives and returns it, one hopes, enhanced.

Any garden we think of installing must take neighborhood into consideration. Madoo has many apertures in its hedges to let in fine trees, no matter how distant. So, too, there are curves and sweeps and castellations and varying levels to let in a good roofline, a provocative chimney, a sweep of lawn or hedgerow. Even a gate. In this way, enlarged and enhanced, it seems part of a broader composition. From one point I see a billowing grove of bamboo. I do not care for forsythia close by, but there are several each spring shimmering on the other side of the hedge. A quite gloomy copse of Norway spruce is another element let in from two houses away, blued a bit more by this little distance and a most welcome amplification to a border of blue caryopteris, Russian sage, annual salvia, and arctic willow. Another neighbor has apple trees whose blooms sift through the hedgerow. Driveways and cars are, of course, inadmissible. When a new road was cut to the south, I raised the hedge level and blotted it out.

Madoo uses no sprays. Discarded through the years have been plants, trees, and bushes requiring such ministrations, replaced by other, hardier, less problematic cultivars. Further, fertilization (outside a teaspoon of lime per clematis each autumn) consists of five truckloads of manure and about sixty bales of mulching hay. Birds are fed throughout the winter and nest throughout the garden, their blueberry, currant, raspberry, and, yes, flower bud pilferings but small tariff for all the insects they destroy. A general salubrious quality has resulted. Good foliage. Fine bloom. A garden in stout heart. Of course, other ministrations are employed. During an overly wet growing season, mulch is lifted from the potager, the better to reduce the slug population. Otherwise, mulches stay down. Divided in three sections, 150 feet of garden clippings and chopped twigs compost in three-year cycles. Other composting is in situ. Foliage unmarred by disease gets chopped and put at the base of the plant from which it is taken, thereby returning precisely the nutrition employed in its growth. Vegetables are washed at an outdoor faucet and the soiled water returned.

Whenever possible, suitable native plant material is used—plants that are garden-worthy and have decent manners, that is. Rampers, overseeders, and overwhelmers are not welcome. Carolina jasmine, clethra, monarda, daisies, gentians, mountain laurel, sweet bay, *grandiflora* magnolia, campion . . . the list is long, very long, and very varied. It does not include native dogwood devastated by disease, nor hemlock now similarly crippled, nor canoe birch, nor . . . Madoo has large plantings of *Ilex glabra*, our native inkberry, a superb substitute for boxwood, tolerating salt-laden winds, less prone to scorch. A stand of pawpaw fruits with increasing generosity, its black-purple blooms an oriental delight. And hollies, ferns, Allegheny pachysandra, milkweed, joe-pye weed. These are mixed with what purists would call "exotics" (and abjure). Ginkgoes, for one. Tree peonies. Rugosas ("our" beach rose is a Japanese import). Montauk daisy (*Chrysanthemum nipponanthemum*). Wanting verticals (a way of italicizing a good effect), I turned from Virginia cedar, which is really a juniper, to the Irish juniper, a more suitable, narrower form.

A healthy, chemical-free garden mandates that one welcome green matter from anywhere, just so long as the cultivars contribute to the general allure, health, and compatibility. That oft-mentioned, soft-lit memory "grandmother's garden" was full of imports and exotics come over from England on the first boat, either as deliberately culled seeds and bundled cuttings or as travelers getting a lift in the bales that livestock munched. Daylilies, chicory, Queen Anne's lace . . .

The Sarvis Tree

THERE IS A flower for every season. My choice for spring is the amelanchier, although with its pale blooms, it does seem negligible in its natural context of marsh and stream margin. But it is a fine small tree nonetheless. Its color is cobwebs or dew on a spiderweb. Its near resembler bloom is the Bradford pear, now so prominent in our streets and parks (and where have they come from, these suddenly so large specimens?) that private gardeners, I think, should turn to the amelanchier, whose looser form makes it suitable for multiple landscape employment. The tight shape of the Bradford restricts its placement in a small plot, and one might well reserve such form for several pillars or posts ramped in vines or a few fastigiate evergreens.

When the amelanchier blooms above rivers and streams, it is called shadblow, for like as not it will be out when shad or other fish come upward to spawn. (Here it is the alewife.) Indians first and then settlers took to its fruit, and it was called Juneberry or Saskatoon. The natives made of the dried fruit ten- or fifteen-pound cakes, chunks of which they would mix with dried, pounded buffalo meat and fat into a highly nutritious, rather classic trail food called berry pemmican. The amelanchier was Thomas Jefferson's favorite. He called it "the Sarvis Tree." The settlers made jam, puddings, jelly, and wine of it, a rather tedious occupation possibly carried out by children or the infirm, for the fruits ripen over a period of three weeks and gathering is a chore. Fruits I say, for berries they are not, botanically, being closer to apples instead, but small. And when, in early spring, the blossoms melted out from their buds, well before the leaves extended, elongating like a run of icewater, amelanchier was the only flower available for funerals, and the plant came to be called the Service Tree. A small branch, a tiny spray, atop the wooden coffin. Grieving in colonial spring could never be lengthy, there was so much else to do, and those many deaths in the early part of the growing year may just have been the easiest to accept, sadness being buried by all the exigent needs of plowing, planting, and tending.

There are some twenty-five species to the genus, most of them native to North America, although there are scattered varieties in Europe, North Africa, and Asia. Loveliness is one reason to plant it, but it is also great food for songbirds. Well pruned, its winter skeleton has grace and modesty and withstands splitting and cracking in storms, for the wood is as hard as persimmon and is still used for the handles of tools.

Of the varieties available, *Amelanchier florida* (also sold as *alnifolia*) and A. *canadensis* turn a fine yellow in autumn, while A. *laevis* is a rich, rich red. The gardener may also wish to plant A. × *grandiflora* (*arborea* and *laevis* crossed), whose leaves are downy and purplish when young and whose flowers are a bit larger. Its cultivar 'Rubescens' has a pink cast. The fruit of all may be eaten by hand, and it is extraordinarily sweet, which is not really much of a contradiction for a funeral flower. As anyone who has felt grief strongly is startled to discover, the aftermath of loss falls in many odd ways through the heart, and contradictions abound.

I have three and am striking cuttings and planting more. They echo the weather most beautifully. Where my garden is situated, spring is largely a matter of mists and fogs more than flowers: mists flat on the fields, mists in from the ocean, mists layering along Sagg Pond and meeting the entirely independent atmosphere of Sagg Preserve. Even my three little ponds will have wisps of such weather in early spring. The Service Tree will come out in counterpoint or replay, the flowers as if exactly colored in the light of the moon or by it, the numinousness carried into daylight, where its light yet dense pigmentation seems half of a full tint, as if halted by the sun. See the Service Tree, if you can, by the light of the moon.

Mountain Laurel

The mountain laurel (*Kalmia latifolia*) is perhaps America's greatest contribution to the gardens of the world. Sadly, no single shrub is so badly planted, so much abused. Because it is shade-tolerant to a fine degree, it seems always to be situated in the darkest old dells. Because it is often seen growing in the wild in happy community with moss, it is generally given the thinnest of soils. It has much stamina, is so patient under extreme neglect that one sees stragglers limping along year after year, with a few pitifully short flushes and disparate patches of undeveloped blooms, where other specimens would have given up. I find this cavalier attitude on the part of the gardener almost approaching the malign.

Now, a flourishing mountain laurel is a buxom, well-mounded, entirely symmetrical shrub. Its natural habit is to send up a great second canopy, on a rich and splendidly crooked reddish trunk, whose flushes will be as exuberantly lime green and as evenly dispersed as its own understory, rising through and above heaps of flower bowls from crown to sides to base. In its grandeur, mountain laurel ought properly to have flag or columbine nearby and woodruff through all, and in the spring, the smallest, most inconspicuous narcissus, iris, or snowdrops—but never that indicator of poor soil, moss. Mountain laurel will keep its dark, shiny foliage whole through winter cold far better than rhododendrons, which flute when the temperature bottoms. Its foliage will be spotless if it is protected from wind. If you cannot give it proper care, do not plant it.

Proper preparation is deep, with humus and peat moss and leaf mold and old manure poured liberally and mixed in the soil. Although mountain laurel is surface-rooted, such preparation will wick up moisture during the dry months and give whatever understory groundcover you want to plant with it sufficient nourishment without interfering with its roots. Having once planted laurel, you must leave its surface entirely undisturbed except for careful weeding as necessary. Each year I top-dress with three or four inches of well-rotted manure atop salt hay. "Top dressing" means exactly that: spread on top of the earth and not mixed in. Mountain laurel is at its best with a half-day's sun or its equivalent accumulated in speckled light. This last illumination will give laurel its best exposure, the light and the dark moving across the polish of the leaves. It means that the overstory will need continual monitoring, continual pruning, so that the light is equal to its growing needs. Where a branch overhead is rigid, it ought to be thinned or lopped entirely. The thicker the branch, the less likely it is to react to the vagaries of air, and the laurel will take too much shade. A supple system overhead is always fine, and one might try laurel under an old, well-pruned apple.

Mountain laurel is made for massing and should never be used as a single specimen. The solitary, brilliantly husbanded mountain laurel will put the remainder of the garden quite in the dumps, for at full growth and mature in habit, it has a peculiarly tropical cast and reminds me of a potted oleander out for the summer air—queer, artificial, definitely unsuitable. Massing must be graceful. Massing does not mean bunching but is closer to being strewn than piled. I would start with two laurels in the same hole and a random dispatchment of four or five others in a full curve collapsing and a single laurel at some distance from the others, like a colonizer striking off alone.

The soil must, of course, be on the acid side, and in our Long Island locale it is. Now, one may test for pH over and over and get entirely different results—pH will vary enormously according to the exuberance of the rainfall, the dryness of the soil, and a multitude of other contributing factors, which will raise or lower it within a range one may think perilous. It is not. It is quite natural. We are on the acid side, and it is quite sufficient for the mountain laurel. Any white magic you may employ by pouring preparations designed to keep acidity within safe bounds is simply bad gardening and dithering fussiness, being short-lived, overly potent, and generally based on green coloring agents so the foliage looks good. Mountain laurel is a slow-growing plant, and all slow growers need slow feeding. An undisturbed mulch, added to annually, will do that. Any hyped-up, abrupt mixture will jar this pattern and make for rapid—too rapid—growth, which will only weaken the plant and reduce its hardiness. One must be patient with the mountain laurel. It rises above gardening seasons, and its aim is perfect performance after a regimen of several years.

The hillside of my childhood had laurels, sad old things under too many oaks. Large but skinny, the laurels had survived nonetheless and gone from plump bushes to scraggles as the oaks closed in. With clearing, their shape and flourish came back. It took five years. Each spring ampler until their glory returned. I used no manure or salt hay then. Oak leaves were sufficient food. And old laurel leaves themselves. The light came slanting morning and afternoon and speckled and flashing at the height of the day. From a distance, when the hill bloomed, all seemed dark until the sun hit the blossoms and the hill swayed with silent, grave whites heading toward, but not quite near, pink.

Note: Don't even think of gathering mountain laurel from the wild. You will incur a fine if you persist—to my mind, one far too low.

Forsythia

Once again I am seriously considering a way to pitch my forsythia. The problem is that it was given me by a friend (they often are) and during her lifetime was impossible to uproot or even move ("You will want it by the door," she firmly said), and now that she is dead and missed, I am loath to do anything at all with it. It has become my leaking outdoor faucet, the stone in the path I never set properly, the jar of something or other I move from the winter refrigerator to the summer one without thought, the odd spice in the odder jar I dust and clean and never open. The forsythia at my winter door has become the voice of conscience.

It is an absolute ass of a color, a greeny-yaller braying insult to the obscure triumph of chartreuse, indisputably wrong for spring, or any other season, for that matter—an irritant of March and April along with inflated, dropsical pansies and sundaes of hybrid azaleas dripping over their mulches of cocoa shells. (Our native azaleas are splendid and rarely used.) The heart of forsythia must be made of aluminum, I think. In a cool spring it blooms on and on. Yet in a warmer one, its performance is no less vulgar, for overly robust foliage then smothers it, green yards of it and all crying "Weed!" It does have a single decent moment when the metallic blossoms drop in little collapses from the stem, sapless and dry and papery dull, coating the ground and making potpourris of little wind-devils across the greening lawn. It is so nice then. Then it seems to rise and sail away into the heart of the spring season, whose hallmark is speed and brevity. All of its other appearances are crude. Its bark is undistinguished. The toothed leaves, although blessedly disease- and insect-free, are as coarse as plantain and look fit only for boiling. Where its branches touch earth—and they do, all the time—they root. Severed roots send up new candidates. Bad and obstinate vines lodge in its base, impossible to eliminate. Mine harbors bittersweet, a crafty honeysuckle married to a dog rose, and a brambly something else that tears at my shirt and smells nasty.

Who wants green in yellow at springtime, when green is what the whole spring world is about? One wants the palest hues, for the light of April is fickle in its modulations and colors everything as it shifts. Daffodils sway down, crocuses close on gray days, hepaticas and violets husband their minute treasures, but forsythia is out on the stem and stuck to it. If it did so in a dark wood one might be grateful, and I have seen a neglected one or two in that sort of situation whose pitiful branches carried a few flowers and seemed charmingly lit. A grand old Chinese elm at my neighbor's has three thin branches of forsythia growing out of a cleft in its trunk, a few feet up from the ground, where all sorts of organic matter has made soil, and there too it looks fine. Here and there one sees an occasional branch poking out of a privet hedge. If I had a meadow going to pot, with grave rusty red cedars (junipers, really) pulling above fawn grass stems and last year's goldenrod, I would plant one in a hollow, behind the junipers, and let its yellow wind and shuttle through the needles. "For*syn*thia," said someone, I forget who, in an alert mispronouncement, as if the bush were chemical and a whiff away from a sneeze. And yet (this "and yet" runs through so much of life) I suppose that I would miss it were it gone entirely or turned very rare. But I also think I wouldn't at all mind the luxury of missing it while it is so much here. Its autumn pose seems to relax its awful energy a bit, and it has a tendency to turn pale ocher or brown, soft and sexy, unless it turns off in spotty fashion, as is too often the case, and then the whole damn bush looks sick.

Forsythia toots from roadside stands and everyone snaps at it like trout at artificial lures. Our being hooked on brightness must clearly be vestigial, but our lives are small affairs in close quarters, and reticence generally is more satisfactory. High-colored blooms annoy as much as hyperactive children and yapping little dogs. As for fast, bright talk, well, it may get the evening going, but true community lies in looks and pauses.

Forsythia gets planted a lot because it is easy to propagate, easy to bag or bundle, easy to ship, stands up under nursery conditions without much toil or trouble, and, once in, does for just about anyone. It is often the garden's first shrub. One can see hedges of it, clipped or not, and singles dotted along front paths, and most often it is wedged among perfectly fine evergreens whose dark backs bring out its glare, framing its horrid pigment like some cash-register gladiolus doubled by the mirror behind. Branches force easily, and in January and February walls of them light up florists'. If you can find some spray picked over a bit by birds who find the flower buds nourishing, you will do the same. But the color won't do indoors either. It simply is not fit for the table.

If I cannot pull mine, for reasons stated, you might yours and generally relieve the neighborhood. Somewhere and awfully close by, someone will have not done so.

If I have my botany right, breeders could have a way out of the dilemma. It might make a fine groundcover. There is an undistinguished dwarf form that might be crossed with the one with variegated leaf and then with the one with purple stems for winter color, and if successful, this new form might be bred to *suspensa* var. *sieboldii*, a fairly acceptable performer. It is a bit like the *wichurana* rose, with long trailing branches, collapsed and crawly at its earthy crown, so that it does well trickling down a hill if there are plenty of rocks and pines in its way. Generally there are not, and things are as gaudy as ever. The English, who delight in clothing trees, sometimes let it go up theirs or even trellis them, but both are poor ideas.

The genus was named for William Forsyth, 1737–1804, superintendent of the Royal Gardens, Kensington. Poor man must be miserable under his monument. His life was otherwise impeccable.

Black Pussy Willow

The black pussy willow (*Salix purpurea*) is a great long-lasting pleasure, not equal quite to the pink or the French hybrid I also grow, yet a shrub whose habit and display are so entirely distinctive as to make such comparison not at all suitable or to the point. It is, of course, not black—there are no black performers in the garden. The mythical black tulip is a shined-up chocolate. 'Bowles' Black' viola, if you are lucky enough to have it, is a rich sooty maroon, and the black pussy willow comes out of that color too but is a bit more saturated with plum. Flowers have got to be bright to attract pollinators.

The *Salix purpurea* I grow is also known as purple osier, and is slender of shoot; they are purpled too, which makes the whole shrub a delight in the winter garden but not that effective in the spring, for the hue seems to get lost in all the brown twigginess around it. *S. purpurea* is also known as basket shrub, although this name seems to apply to other species as well, the willow family at large being as inter-threaded as the woven containers their wythes make. Reading up on this willow, I have gotten lost many times tracking it down, and I find that my sources do not even agree on just how high it ultimately gets. One lists its mature form at ten feet and another at seven to nine, which is quite vague. The way mine is developing, I will be pleased if it tops at six feet. But my plant is not entirely in the open, so I cannot claim to be a judge. However, I estimate from the lengths of its urgent young shoots and their transient lives that six, perhaps even seven feet is all I may expect, and certainly not ten for the grown form.

One of the nicest traits of this plant is a tendency to bush or dress itself out at the bottom before long tapers go upward. Actually, that's all it did for me the first year—to the point where I thought I might pitch it, for it remained in scraggle and gave but few catkins or pussies. Since then, however, it has been generous. The buds have the usual single scales, but they wear them nicely until they peak, and they curve around the stem with hats on, giving two shades of dark and light brown. Each is not a swollen catkin but a rather elongated one, and it has a refreshingly wild quality. My sources rally here to say that the shrub has escaped from cultivation in many places. This is hardly surprising, for willows are generally found in wet places and along streams, and their easily rootable, breakable twigs would thus float on spring freshets to lodge and hold somewhere else. My books also say that they have "a tendency to run wild." Generally this indicates a heavy seeder, and willows are, but such fine ones that they are not viable for very long, and one must think that man as well as streams has broken off branches and carried them home and lost one or two in the process. Certainly the shrub doesn't colonize by underground runners, which is a great relief. It will, however, root readily if you will only bend a low branch to the earth and moor it there under a rock or with just enough earth to hold it. Anything used for basket-making has got to be pliant.

I can see it as a hedge quite readily, and this might be a solution for anyone working near the North Atlantic, where hedging is limited to growers able to take wind and salt. My arctic willows (another prime candidate for the windbreak) are not affected by them, and neither, for that matter, is the hybrid pussy willow, which might make a hedge as fine as Russian olive, silvered on the underside of the leaf just like the olive but more responsive to moving air and so more interesting and less stolid in a long line. I think it might be worth trying on steepish hillsides, for all willows are quite mat-rooted and superior candidates for erosion control. Any little gully or wash might do too. Or a mixed planting of arctic willow and osier willow, the arctic willow's stems as flexible in winter as they are the rest of the year, shuttling back and forth in the wind, Nile green to young fawn and mixing with the rubbed purples of the osier's shoots. And perhaps a few American hollies stuck among them, possibly protected enough by the tangle, giving tantalizing glimpses of their bright red berries.

Members of the willow family are great users and transpirers of water, and this purification process has always made a willow welcome around a cesspool for its sanitary effect. Unfortunately, the weeping willow will throw roots in the drains and tangle them up. A clump planting of purple osier, which has a lighter root run, might be a more satisfactory solution with less fuss.

Almost Spring

Prolonged cold is odorless. There is only chimney smoke. The smell of oil or gas or wood. Early thaws too are without smell, if they are brief. If only slush were odorous, each mound spiced! I think the odor might be something in the large assortment of emanations from roots, a smell of nameless turnings in the woods—burrow smells, hole smells, tunnel smells, smells where small things chewed through roots to make tubular chambers for communication and flight. Without odor, winter has no weight at all, and perhaps that is to the good, that it stays light in the air, but months of it make for such a huge, unfilled space.

By late February, I begin to find smells again, in small curves where the sun has been striking windlessly, patches where bulbs are beginning to grow, patches where growth greens are replacing refrigerated ones, patches that, if I had a mind to mark them, would make wavy, detailed maps of warmish microclimates in the garden. There are many, beyond the obvious one of soil next to buildings. Soil adjoining heavy stones, for one. Soil beneath the pebbled drive, for another, always apt to warm sooner if the stones are dark, and stay warm longer than soil beneath white pebbles or soil not under pebbles. Edges of driveways thus are perfect for snowdrops. And underneath heavy shrubberies one might have shoals and fingering peninsulas of bulbs late in the season, for here ice will stay and stay and extend the bloom of the earliest snowdrops well into tulip time. With ample spring winds, sunlight will filter down through shrub-sway enough for them to mature and form buds in their bulbs for the following year, although this is always a bit of a risk.

At this time of year, I start raking. And raking. Twigs from the path of the mower, leaves from the drive. Enormously cold, soaking wheelbarrows of leaves go to mulch pines and rhododendrons, mountain laurels and, of course, continually greedy yews.

On days like this I might go toward the tool shed and then put off cleaning it. Why waste the day? I feel not at all inclined to be cooped up again. So I go back to the long winter driveway, with stepladder, shears, and saw, and start cresting privet at about seven feet, lowering it to give shrubs on its other side a bit more sun. A bit like sweeping a huge curtain from a window, or repainting a wall. When all leaf out, the grouping will be seen for the first time against the panel of privet.

As soon as their branches are trimmed enough to let the fuel truck in, that is. With two houses, two studios, I have to make arrangements for deliveries and maintenance: a tank for fuel, another for gas, ugly meters for electricity, a trash area convenient for pickup where I would rather have a beech. Plumbing lines seem always to burst when the garden is at peak, electric conduits fuster out underground, and then there are poles leading from Main Street to the summer house and two well covers marked for lifting and two covers for the cesspools and cords of wood at each studio. Traditional garden plans never include such interruptions, dating as they do from days when labor was cheap and nearly everything was toted, whether a cup of tea from a kitchen hidden away or coal in buckets from a dark unknown cairn. The truly sensible arrangement would be to have all such unavoidables under one roof, adjoining a tool shed or garage in a decently designed structure bowered with roses and connected to the house by a long book-lined hall. Somehow it will be done when sense comes calling at the entire home system, in which everything will be recycled. As yet it is a scheme full of error. It will begin when a tiny solar panel no larger than my fingernail is cheap and marketed cheaply. For now, I find that an oil furnace is simple. I have lived with coal fires and kerosene fires and wood fires, and they none of them are worth the cost of personal labor. As for solar systems in the Northeast, with all of those fans upstairs and slag heaps in the basement, all that sense of water percolating through the walls? No. For me, large double- or triple-paned windows are enough.

SEEDS

OF THE UNCOUNTED THOUSANDS I have bought, the first ones were, if I recall, 'Red Sparkler' radish, five cents, the envelope glossy, impossibly but alluringly colored, a bouquet of them thrust directly at the viewer, root ends clean and glowing, directions on the obverse and as simple as a highway traffic sign. The Burpee Seed Company, Philadelphia, Pa. It seemed all nice seeds came from Burpee, still in business decades later, but not with the large and various selections they used to advertise.

Now there are more specialized firms, and one takes only a few from each, so that examples are on my desk from Park's, Shepherd's, the Cook's Garden, Heirloom Seeds, Johnny's, the impossibly costly and stingy Thompson and Morgan, Stokes, Tomatoes Only, Pinetree Gardens . . .

I have them on hand now, all that I have ordered—or overordered, I should say—and will probably order more. The box that keeps them out of the light is having difficulty with its lid. I know that I will come across still another lettuce boasting never-halting sweetness and snap even through summer heats, a lettuce slow to bolt, one that might even winter over. But no matter, lettuce seeds stay viable for at least five years.

Most of the little fascicles are now unillustrated, or only in black and white, frequently on fawn-colored packages of recycled paper, much more intricately labeled, sometimes as to country of origin, rates of germination, date of packaging, cultivation suggestions—a minicourse in agriculture. Rarely a price. Sometimes a Latin name. Sometimes phonetic pronunciation. Racks of them, a pretty dour affair.

Where is Mistress Mary? She, the perfect emblem of rural arcadia, with edible raspberry cheeks and cherry lips and hair of cornsilk, blue eyes so very blueberry blue, bent over a border with a watering can from which hyphens of black type arched, which you knew to be water, all under a cloud-flecked sky of blue sitting on the roof of a little cottage. Five cents. Then ten. Then an alarming twenty or twenty-five, the price rising from the base of the envelope, aiming for the sky and then higher still until the numbers fled the envelope. Seeds became pelleted for easier sowing or treated for fungus with some nasty stuff whose color came off on your fingers.

I have a promising series of mescluns from the Cook's Garden, a mesclun bed being a lazy approach to a salad that is piquant and vigorous. The makings for any such salad are already sprouting in a well-furnished vegetable garden, but spread out, the fennel tops and young arugula there, various lettuce and endive types here, and chards, mustards, young parsley, and chives in as many other locations. Beet greens are as mesclun as pea shoots, mesclun being really anything young and tasty.

I've got notes on all the packages, both vegetables and flowers: early and late sowings for the greenhouse, early and late outdoor sowings, those that have to be filed to break dormancy, those that have to be soaked overnight, or chipped, sanded, or filed for similar reasons, those to be planted in late August when nights are cool, those to be planted in situ, those to be transplanted once or twice, some for rows in the potager for August lift and plunge, those to be acclimated in the cold frame . . . And then those that are annual, perennial, biennial.

My notebook has the orders in duplicate, pasted on the verso page for reference. Some are marked "BO" for back orders; a few have that sad and dismaying note "Sorry, sold out." But rarely, for I order early. If I can restrain myself, which is quite unlikely, I will begin planting in the greenhouse in earliest March.

From Shepherd's I have ordered six deep-containered flats that might just eliminate transplanting, and I would like so much to see whether this is true. Further, little Mistress Mary is a most persuasive image, and even though she is now absent from the packages, I still see her insouciance, she of the bows and the watering can, the winding path, the little cottage, and that moist blue sky of a coming gardening year.

Today's little packages of seeds seem to be never enough or far too much. They seem intended for some unreasonable prototype patch a computer determined and are about as adaptable to one's personal needs, and whatever the number, no amount will be of any use unless the row or bed is pulverized to a fine tilth and made as level as a billiard table. The seeds go on this without rolling or falling into what for them would be ravines. If they are fine and tiny, they may then be merely pressed into the earth with the flat of the hand. Or a board will do. When larger, a sifting of soil. You may wish to fill a large jar with fine covering soil and poke holes in its lid. Use it to flour over the row of the bed. And that is that. There is nothing wrong, however, with a more generous approach, which is to overseed and then transplant the results. With care, even beets can be so handled. If not, you must thin them out, and this is a hard chore. Larger seeds, like beans and peas, may be pressed into the bed or the row at the proper distance with a finger to the correct depth; generally this is two to four times the seed's diameter, but this will depend on the weight of your soil. The heavier it is, the less deep the seed goes.

The planting of seeds is very definitely a personal affair, and much depends on the gardener's hand. No one can tell you exactly how. It is the pinch of salt in a recipe.

Notes

To look over notes made the twenty-ninth of March of 1999 is to see them as so much the common traffic of early spring as to be a kind of paradigm of the season. Notes of previous years echo this: "While working in the morning, three paintings going and one about to be launched, Carlos plugs in a long extension cord and sets about sawing off the rotted ends of the two gateposts. Coatless, I go out to see them installed in their new situation and am delighted to see them work so well. They are now at the curve of one of the perimeter walks through the meadow, the one through mixed young bushes and trees underplanted with what goldenrod lodged there ending the first small meadow, making it a cul-de-sac, and a walker will come upon it but not all at once. A decent effect, not at all grand, no, but the big feeling a gate always gives.

"Carlos vetoes my idea of moving some blueberries to a stretch in front of the summer house. 'It's nice open,' he says, and saves me much work and stays me from the great error of crowding out the whole effect of this other open meadow. Although in their maturity they would not be very high and I was of a mind to plant them in drifts, it would have the planted look I do not wish here and am instead putting in overflow chicory, milfoil, and daylily. Where the blueberries now are is perhaps the windiest point in the garden and overrun with rabbits, so that what plants survive will be slow in maturing and it is another area of my plot whose effect will take years. I will help push them along, when the wind loses its ocean chill, by increasing the depth of manure and peat moss I spread around each of the three hundred bushes last autumn, which has settled low at their basing. Went then back into the studio.*

"At eleven began spading the far triangle of the vegetable garden, spading double spits, and laid a small path for the first bed but then hated the look and removed the setts. Laid them flat on the low retaining wall of the silver, gray, white garden, leaving some setts out and so making small alcoves where I put three pottery lanterns. Intended to be awfully French Intensive in my spading. Looks, however, come first. As a small sop for the lapsed effort, I found no impaction at all at the deepest level but toiling earthworms, and who can better turn soil than they? Lunch, nap, more spading. Staked out the corner where twelve yews will be placed, making the inner garden more separate from the main path. Enlarged the path adjoining the vegetable garden, moving blue Nepalese columbine further in among the woodruff and straw.

"A package from Wayside at the post office when I went for the second mail. *Rosa lutea* entirely in leaf, so will keep it in its pot indoors until roses outside are in large leaf. And a *Franklinia*, a small tree far too tender for our climate, but

---

*The rabbits nibbled the blueberries, each and every one.

I think I have a pocket as protected from the prevailing winds as if a high stone wall had been built there. And did I say that I tossed mullein seedlings from the vegetable garden over the fence and pitched some soil on top of them, which is a lazy way of transplanting indeed, but the mullein came out in clumps and so ought to do. I aim for a long stand behind the fence—fat and gray furry leaves with yellow pyres of bloom August to September. Staked out some lovage, horseradish, and garlic chives to be moved to a new bed next to the toolhouse where they will mix with bergamot and sage and give it a nice random look. Got in a row of pod peas, one of spinach, one each yellow keeper onions and red. Wind high, cold increasing. I went to several nurseries to look once again for American holly and *Rhododendron maximus*. Holly unobtainable, except in specimen size. The blue hybrids are fine in their way, but the foliage singes and needs burlapping. The rhododendron too came only in specimen size.

"In the late afternoon, letters and sorting out seeds, dividing the envelopes into planting groups: earliest spring, later spring (but before last frost), frost free, warm soil, summer succession, and late summer for fall crops. In the evening, lined out lettuce seedlings in one large pan. Then turned to the garden books of Thomas Jefferson: 'The motion of my blood no longer keeps time with the tumult of the work . . . my farm, my family & my books call me to them irresistibly . . . there is not a sprig of grass that shoots uninteresting to me.' "

PLANT PORTRAITS II

False Indigo

To call baptisia "false indigo" is a bit of a slur on its character, as if its aspirations were toward masquerade. Although it patently isn't indigo, it was indigo enough when the real thing wasn't around and its color was a perfectly acceptable substitute. Rattlebush is its other name, and this is a bit better, but horsefly weed is putting aspersion on it again, since it mostly blooms in June, when bees, not flies, are pitched on it, drinking heavily. It is a greatly undervalued border plant and a native plant rather skimpily documented. One top source I have gives twenty-five distinct species in North America, and another, equally learned, between forty and fifty. Two of its varieties, as if to cover the lapses of scholarship that underline its dubious position, are *confusa* and 'Exaltata'. *B. australis* is the one to get if you like blue.

I found my first at a local nursery and since then have grown others from collected seed. The plant I started with over twenty-five years ago has never been divided and is entirely content in its undisturbed state, slowly enlarging, becoming more massive, blooming every year. The Greek part of its name, *baptisis,* means to dip or bathe (the root is black with a yellow center), and the seeds, which were used as an emetic and an antiseptic, rattle quite loudly in their casings and are sufficiently ornamental to be left drying above the pea-leafed bush, where the sound will tell you on a still August day that air is moving nonetheless. I like to leave the stalks all winter, too. That the plant is leguminous is another boon; nodules on its roots fix nitrogen back into the soil. Any soil. Common treatment and full sun are what it takes. It is a plant of the prairies and a perennial of sandy woods and will take to the banks of rivers, but I would assume small ones, ones that may dry up or sink radically during hot weather, for I think it prefers dry soil or at least soil that is highly drained.

My major one grows in full sun and dry soil. (I have just planted others in hotter but less dry spots on the terrace, in spaces below the single line of terrace blocks that hold soil washing from higher beds.) Its pealike sprouts and pea-colored leaves settle into lupine foliage shapes and darken by midsummer, making a stable mound of a plant fine for a bed of blue-green foliage undercolored by gray. The central stems can be two, three, or four feet high, depending on whether you have the cream, the yellow, or the blue variety, but all outer stems curve out of the center toward the light, reaching toward the ground, so that it makes for an undisturbed symmetry throughout the growing season.

Baptisia is the sort of plant that can screen something low and unsightly, like a bulge of concrete where cement has oozed from a foundation. If I had a large, highly colored stone, I would place it near the plant's center so that part of the fine architecture of the branches might show. I think it would be fine as a low border hedge, for it never jumps its bounds, and it sockets well into a walkway bed you might want to color blue or gray-blue, perhaps with santolina or bunches of flag. *Baptisia australis* blooms with the lupines in June, and the cream and yellow ones later. These might all be combined into a broad avenue of moundy plants. If spaced properly, ground huggers could sweep around their stable formalism. The various creeping thymes would be suitable, being blue in cast or gray and liking the same sort of hot, dry situation.

Rattle-bags

Campion definitely belongs in a good garden. It is a wave-breaking mass remindful of that other well-known gadabout of field and meadow, bouncing Bet or Mary-by-the-gate, and is as persistently nostalgic as a faded postcard. Frothy, and in some species sticky (the stem as well as its calyx), campion can be erect in its growing habit, or it is an acceptable toppler, or even mildly climby, with a slight tendency toward dropsy. Some do well in the rock garden and have been cultivated for it. Its Latin name is *Silene*, after Silenus, an eager follower of Bacchus, depicted as "covered in foam." It is an immensely large, worldwide family, and my memory gets set adrift with all its varieties, and they merge in my mind. The nodding catchfly is one of these, for I swear I've seen it here, although it is an escape from Europe and found only on Mount Desert Island in Maine and on Staten Island in New York City.

I grow bladder campion (*Silene cucubalus*), or is it that I only think I do? On clear or strongly milky days it closes, but some stay open in thick cloudy weather. It is fully open only at night, ravishing under flashlight, its scent alert yet confined, very much like that of an old but clean bit of furniture polish. Out of the mass will tumble two small petals—a moth of the same color, for that is the way it is pollinated. It looks like white pewter, and like pewter plate, it is a good mixer both as accent and as underliner, throwing other foliage into significant relief and blooming with skillful, abundant reticence. Its dull leaves are longish and also like metal. It nourishes in a small area of soil, feeding daintily, so there is never fuss about encroachment. Seedlings pull up without difficulty. A fine take from the hedgerow.

According to one of my sources, the young shoots "are said to be eaten by the poor folk of England as a substitute for asparagus; they taste something like green peas." Which makes them, to my mind, no substitute at all. Peas are peas.

A whorl of four indented petals is set above a bladder of striped whitish green traced with darkness of brown on a spiked stem. In these sacs the seeds set. The scattering is copious, and its sound has given the plant names such as bull rattle or rattle-bags, snappers, devil's rattlebox, and, curiously, maiden's tears. It *does* sound something like pouring granulated salt. I prefer one of its other calls: spattling poppy.

Bladder campion will be where the highway mowers don't go. I waited for a heavy rain to gather it, taking some of the home earth to encourage the roots, and I cut the plants down to stay the shock. I set them in with plenty of water and some rigged-up shade to give them a chance. Here was another use for hot caps, with large holes snipped at the top to let the heat out. But it was better when I marked a stand and gathered seeds still in the bladder, then scattered them as I wished. The performance was without rehearsal and had the randomness they should display. I left a solitary one (was it the catchfly?), for it seemed like a lone soldier on reconnoiter and I hoped for an army. I haven't seen it since.

Once in the garden, the bladder campion has become a regular and not an adjunct, doing well in any sort of weather, any sort of soil, May to September. Rabbits pass it by, but like people in museums who don't give a sou for a postcard, rabbits forage and gather not.

Plume Poppy

Whether you call it plume poppy or bocconia or macleaya or greater celandine, you will be naming a not-much-used plant (which is a pity), one that is a roaring perennial whose form and rate of growth suggest an exuberant young tree. Colored as brightly as an aspen, with a trunk much like some silvery, shivery bamboo, plume poppy (*Macleaya cordata*) is a stalwart gallant all about providing accent, courteous to the health of neighboring plants while being a community all by itself. It is one of those astonishing performers in the herbaceous border capable of changing the elevations of one's plant collection early on in the season and then continuing up and up, according to water supply and nutrition and how assiduous one is in thinning the colony.

And just what is it? I find that it is listed in herbals by reason of the juice of its leaf stems. It will stain your hands saffron. It will take care of insect bites. It grows in China, says one reference book, but another says that it grows in Japan too, while yet another lists it as a denizen of Central and South America. Whatever its point of origin, it is wonderful that it is here, and however vague source books may be about its home or its lineage, it is never listed without the adjective *handsome,* to which I would not hesitate to add *elegant,* for that is what it undeniably is.

A wonder of a plant, nearly eight feet in height and, placed properly in the garden, of splendid effect. I like it opened up and do quite a bit of stem-stripping (hence, saffron hands) in order to see the fine silken sheen of its blue-green but nearly silver stem. Its leaves will work too, with downy undersides of palest felt. Occasionally a breeze or water from the sprinklers will turn the leaves so the felty undersides grab at the light. It is then a most satisfactory arrangement of grays. It flowers in enormous panicles, a bit like a grass, and the inflorescence is modest, not showy, and is a fine furry cream, at times brown.

Plants are one way to acquire specimens, but you might try seeds too, or root divisions. Although it can be invasive, shoots pull up readily, particularly if the soil is wet. And that is that for its cultivation. It will be back in place, tidy and well mannered. A joy. As high as it will get, it requires no staking. It was named for Paolo Boccone, a seventeenth-century Sicilian botanist, and I do hope he is happy in the honor of being the first, for the glory has somewhat been taken away. So marvelous a plant acquired another parent and was later named for Alexander Macleay, secretary of the Linnean Society and colonial secretary of New South Wales. So let us say bocconia.

Now, for mine. I have a colony that began by a door in the inner garden. There is nothing finer than looking through this little grove of brilliant trunks—at times as shiny as a jet of water, at times not liquid at all but a bright yet dulled new metal (like a sheet of steel between polishings)—glimpsing other sections of the garden through them, as though one were coming out of a house in the woods and then a meadow began. Certain plants are so compelling that by looking hard at them, the eye is momentarily sharpened and will then look well and hard at other parts of the garden, refreshed and more aware of even the littlest things. Very much as seeing a fine painting in some collection gives one an awareness of seductions elsewhere on the walls.

Broom

Broom is always on the off side of green, even when mature, as if half its life were in reserve. There is something mythic about it, something edged in the gray of an ancient ambiguous dawn. It is, to all purposes of the raw eye, leafless, sipping at the light from a febrilated apparatus that, swamped by huge rains, might look perfectly comfortable beneath the sea. A green gone blurry down in the water. Its structure is like a huge nerve, with extensive dendrites and ganglia. As much as it seems to come out of legends and from the past, it yet hits at bionic futures, for it is a stripped-down, efficient, and withal highly successful plant. It is a reminder that as much as we may design and design, the new succeeds only when it alludes to the past, forgotten though it might be, for reasons not necessarily inherently valid. Good form is not merely elegant. Physicists speak of beautiful symmetry, and mathematicians value proportion.

Broom seems lifted from the page, a pressed twig gathered by an unknown plant collector, label lost, expedition forgotten, uninhibited by documentation. It is an analogue to the Southwest's chamiso, another plant as good as a ghost. Contemporary gardeners would be wise to pick up on broom, for its offerings, like its heart, bulk large and various. It might form the core of a contemporary garden around which other plantings navigate.

A stone might be in its making, broom seems so slow—a turtle's shell responding to the light and the warmth of spring. It looks as if a mineral dust had gotten into its phloem and were carried to the tops, yet this inert aspect is so self-abnegating it isn't particularly noticeable. A birdlike shoot will flush at the base. And others, smaller, until it blooms. Mostly it stoops and wanders down toward the earth as if trying to hide from its destiny in the air. As it ages it twists and flails. ("Let me in, let me in," the old man of legend cries to the earth.) It is a big piece of dried star moss, beating on and on.

The scent of its blossoms drives bees frantic—an odor supported by dark, sharp chords of bitterness, like wet bark under oleander or honeysuckle above the steaming earth of southern pitch pines. When broom is on pour, there is no room for any other garden odor, for it will mask them all; as deeply as you might search for the scent of magnolia or lilacs, you will never discern either when the air is full of broom. It will rasp the sense of smell and leave it a bit disdainful of anything less fierce and independent. Yet as much as its odor predominates, the shape, habit, and behavior of the plant are most condign to mixing. It is a perfect counterpart to nearly everything. I think that a solid meadow of it with white rugosa roses and then autumn asters might be a splendid thing with, yes, perhaps some lime-green daffodils to begin the composition or, better, *poeticus narcissi* (narcissus, daffodil; daffodil, narcissus—let us call them one thing, not two). Or a whole field of just broom with tall yellow lilies coming through. Anything tall will do with it, like verbascum and eremus or birch, Irish juniper and grasses. But I like it with holly too, for it takes to bushy forms as well, and mixing them with red- and yellow-twigged dogwood would be the making of a damned fine winter garden. Or a single great old broom in a field. Just that. I saw a magnificent specimen at the gate to the water mill in, yes, our neighboring village, Water Mill. Yellow. I trust it is there still. I have two oldish ones in a spot where they seem a bit fagged and fudge the clean-lined effect I am after there, but I have been having this terrible time now for three years running, trying to decide whether to risk moving them, and I probably won't. Older specimens just don't take to it. If they weren't so curious there, looking like rudiments of an older garden, I wouldn't hesitate to give them a solid two-thirds cutback (immediately after they bloom, which is the proper time for such drasticness). I may. I will have to get myself into an awfully furious mood, I fear, and perhaps an hour spent trying to eradicate bittersweet and dog rose will set me up.

I have many and am still planting others—brooms, that is. The roots must be gently disengaged from the swirly pattern they take on in their containers, for without this care, they will forever grow concentrically as if never depotted, their bound feet good only for tottering. Roots not gently directed out from the center eventually strangle the plant.

Broom would be splendid on a front lawn, instead of the front lawn. Perhaps I would stick in some birch. All winter it would allude to growing without the obtuseness of pachysandra or pine, which are too dark for the job. In spring, the expanse would seem like the wind itself gone green again, a paradigm of all spring blows that simmer down and begin to blur the petals and young leaves before going out in summer. There are many varieties to choose from in both of the genera we call broom, *Genista* and *Cytisus*.

First Garden

❧

I'VE SEEN my first garden for the last time. After much family doubt and misgiving, the property, a country house on a lake, was finally sold, and the contents of it were to be divided among relations, an aunt and cousins chiefly, but first choice was to be mine. A mixed day, echoed by the weather. I left Sagaponack in mist and then rain and drove through Manhattan to the Ramapos in more fog. These low, soft preliminaries to the Catskills were touched by autumn, trees running with ruddied Virginia creeper and whole hills of lemon birch still in full leaf. And then the sun came out and I was there. I found that my first garden had gone back to woods, which had really been my original intention, although not so much so, and that secondary growths of oaks and sassafras were again mixed in with mountain laurel and native white rhododendrons in exactly the same way they had been when the family first took charge of the land forty-odd years ago.

Years had been spent pruning oaks, thinning out saplings to let light in. Bare areas received more mountain laurel and rhododendron, and copses were made of hemlock and andromeda. More exposed patches of scarcely interrupted light received wildflowers lifted from surrounding meadows. Lining one side of the badminton court at the base of the hill, I made a long rock garden with lady's slipper, ground pine, partridgeberry, and native azaleas. A small lawn ended in a pool sunk below the exposed roots of a beech shadowed by sweet pepperbush, and a more-or-less formal flower border backed by yews took off from it. And then there were more steps, more lawn, and then the lake, the house near its edge banked with rhododendrons. Many levels. Many fieldstone steps. Walls made by my father. Roundabouts and alcoves of stone for sitting; docks, bathhouse, tool house. A nice coherent unit with easy flow and little surprises of flowers and shrubbery of a more exuberant nature as paths turned and alcoves widened; a cocoa-colored *Magnolia lilliflora* that bloomed in autumn as well as in spring, and boxwood clipped and a witch hazel trained in a nicely patterned canopy over a standing swing.

A garden shaped and reshaped to meet the changing needs of a family, the house altered and then altered again, a road cut through the hill for easier access to the car; for a few years a vegetable garden from which my first radish was pulled, gravely cut in four by my mother and pronounced superb. A garden with problems of deer and muskrats and much falling in of shorefront. A garden over stubborn cold clay and granite outcropping fertilized with canal muck from cleanings of onion fields in Florida, New York. And much fragrant leaf mold. A garden of tremendously heavy leaf fall when autumn raking seemed to go on forever. I spent all the summers, weekends, and vacations of my childhood there, combing the hills and the nearby swamps for native material, learning much and becoming canny about extracting fine growth from such difficult soil.

What feelings I have about it all seem curiously in reserve, as if it were some kind of laboratory workshop of an apprenticeship that is not over, where fumbling remains intrinsic and next season is more important than the present one. It seems to me now, however, that the garden had been at all times already there. A natural wood that perhaps could have taken a few paths and been left at that, except for the family living areas set in the rich, involved green—for so much native raw energy ought to have been honored and let be. I was pleased to see that my imposition on it was temporary and grieved to learn that the property will be chopped into building plots. I can see fastidious lawns and swimming pools and an awful sameness with all of the trees gone, and I hope I will not pass that way again. I took some of my earliest tools, a rake and a hoe and a shovel, and that is nice and continuous. I am taking the sound of my father chipping stone with a trowel and setting a final fine rock on top of one of his great walls. I am taking the voice of my mother congratulating me on my radish. Upstairs in the house I am still pressing red swamp maple leaves into wax on a sheet of glass and tilting it on the windowsill so the light comes through. I am visiting all the gardens and nurseries of the area, talking and learning, a long weed of a child begging cuttings, nursing robins, getting lost in a boat in a wild hailstorm. I am painting pictures on old rusty trays one rainy summer on the porch while Mother is heaving sighs over *Kristin Lavransdatter* and my father is playing solitaire. I am ignoring my brother as usual and paying no attention to what he is doing, which is making a model of the *Bounty*. I am getting up and playing an old record of Galli-Curci's. It stops raining and I discover that of the three cardinal plants I lifted from the edge of the marsh, only one is beginning to stalk with bloom and it is in the wettest hollow of the rock garden, and so I move the other two near it. “I think more roses near the bathhouse would be nice,” says my mother. Tomorrow, if the weather clears, we will go to Warwick and pick some out.

That last day was exactly the time we would have roamed the hills for clusters of wild grapes and then begun the annual chore of making jelly, taking baskets and climbing over rocks, calling like wildfowl when we found a low vine. Green grapes added made the jars that much tarter and tastier. When I left the house for the last time, a young vine on the hill was just beginning to bear.

Fairies

Sometime in the early part of the nineteenth century a certain tale of the fairies' ring crossed the Atlantic on a wooden ship, in steerage. In the retelling, the Irish and Scots added dew to the story, and it arrived on our shores in this form: If on a walk through the woods you come across a perfect circle of greenest moss and this circle is surrounded by white, white mushrooms, you have come upon the fairies' ring. If you wait until Midsummer's Eve when the dew is falling, you may enter the ring and lie down on the moss and wish for beauty. But if you stand on the moss in the middle of the ring through all of that long, magical night, you may wish without end, and all of your wishes will be granted. And the story goes on about one young boy who did, and all the things, miserable and happy, that happened to him as a result.

I first heard the story when I was nine from a proud, tall, red-haired teacher of poetry, and it has never left my head. Odd though I thought her (she often grinned at nothing at all and laughed when the occasion was empty of humor), I was convinced of its truth. I began my wish list, and through the years I have continued to do so, for no night is long enough to recite all one's dreams, and I believe in being prepared. That the list has changed through the years is only autobiography, but its content has always hovered around gardening, more or less, for this activity seemed to me then and seems to me now to be most appropriate for such a grand and magical moment. For my first gardens, in New York City and New York State, I wanted better soil; for the one in Vermont, leveler ground; for the one in Maine, a longer frost-free season; and for the two in New Mexico, rain, of course. Now, out here, on the alluvial outwash flats of Bridgehampton loam, soil is fine and earth is level, rain is not an issue, nor do I find the season too short. But there are other major considerations.

I find that I definitely need another arm and another hand, preferably ambidextrous. At Camburi Beach, north of São Paulo, I spoke to a distinguished plastic surgeon. "Can you help me?" I asked. Looking at my face, he answered, "It will be difficult, but I think I can." I then passed him my sketch. "I think I can't," he said. I had presented him with two possibilities. This arm I needed came either from the center of my chest or from the middle of my back over my head like some sort of crane and was, of course, longer than the two I already have. He said that this was beyond his skill or the skill of any other plastic surgeon he knew. "At the present time we have no way of doing this, there being no requests for this sort of procedure," he said. "It is unique. It is impossible. But who knows?" And then he smiled encouragingly. Brazilians hate to say no. I knew that I would have to apply to the fairies.

Further, as far as my garden stands, I realize that I must have another acre in order to flesh it all out and amplify its thrust. (I do need, and feel that I cannot do without, a very long alley of trees.) Perhaps two acres. Things have gotten built up around me, though, and there is no more room for horticultural sprawl. But the fairies could come to the rescue by bringing me two acres all broken up and floating on several levels, with wonderful staircases and ladders leading to and from them. (If a garden can be described as a succession of rooms, then why can't it, like a house, have a succession of floors?) Light could enter slantwise from the sides and water come down in a series of little waterfalls. Incas made magnificent fields on the steepest sides of the Andes, brought in conduits of water from far away, and grew more than two hundred varieties of potatoes, in all sorts of strange shapes and colored black and purple and orange and blue.

I have complete confidence that the fairies will come to my aid in this, and I will then reward them by planting a lake on my enlarged plot and surrounding it with sward and on the sward placing a cow and from that cow taking the milk and from the milk the cream and putting it out in little bowls on every doorstep (I have ten). No matter that I might be feeding cats and raccoons, just as long as the bowls are empty each morning. Fairies come in any shape, not just Godmother or Tooth.

Lamentably, current technology doesn't seem to be interested in lost tools. They're even wandering in outer space. Fairies could equip them with beepers so that one might hear, "This is your Cape Cod weeder, lost in the long border next to 'Madame Isaac Pereire,' where I see, by the way, thrips!" And in morning, voices of a more general sort the fairies daily might deliver. "Heavy dew drying. Wind from a bit south of the west. Soon three dandelions will blow. Stop them. Harvest your beets. They are at their sweetest. Slugs are sliming toward the Cos, and the first cleome has opened. Do as you wish, but I recommend striking box cuttings now, for next winter will do in many of them. A plump brown bat circled the new box all last night and just might settle in, and Charles, your favorite garden snake, has just shed his skin and needs to be admired. All in all, the garden is in acceptable fettle, but *Phlomis cashmeriana* will soon be in a deplorable state. Look at it and find out why. The clue is in the lower leaves. Oh, the green heron is back on the bridge, but don't worry, the goldfish and the frogs are safe. He's the world's worst fisher. More later, come sunset."

And the same soft, sweet little voices would come to me whenever I gave tours. "No, do not say that that is the plant whose name you can never remember. You know perfectly well what its name is. And you will remember. Don't, however, be so overjoyed that you forget three others. And do not cover your lapses with 'Botany is the fine art of insulting flowers in Latin.' It isn't yours and everyone has heard it. Read Liberty Hyde Bailey again. Did you see the lady in blue? Took a seedhead from the Nepalese columbine. Glare. Or, better, say, 'If any of you want any seeds from anything, just leave its name and yours as you leave and I will send it. Don't forget your address.' She'll never pilfer again."

And I think of those tiny, industrious hands plying their wonderful ways each night, weeding, wiping mildew off the railings, deadheading flowers, picking up fallen leaves, growling at visiting dogs (nothing deadlier to tulips than the tail of a Labrador), making dew more abundant when drought is high, unkinking hoses, hastening compost, making sure the wheelbarrows' tires are full, desqueaking all rolling things, sharpening shears, shining windows, filling ponds, sweeping terraces . . . Faucets would never drip, nor watering cans rust, nor sprinklers stall or topple. Blues would follow whites just when and as I planned. All invasions of honeysuckle, bittersweet, and thistles would end, and August's bottoming would never strike.

And the same soft, sweet little voices would come to my ears and tell me that if, on the second of July, at exactly two in the morning, I did a perfect back flip, I would need only to stare at Japanese beetles to turn them into Baroque pearls. And the same receipt, but one requiring three flips, would work for ticks. And the voices would whisper "Roses," and I would go out to the rose walk and see perfect blooms on thornless stems above dark blue unblemished foliage.

The voices would speak and I would heed them all and all good things would come to my garden. Or should I say come to their garden, for the garden would no longer be mine.

I don't think that I want to have a fairy-run, fairy-managed garden.

As a matter of fact, it is out of the question.

WEATHER

Our Climate

IF YOU SHOULD TAKE a plane from East Hampton and go around the area, the issue of our peculiar climate will become clear. From the air, the north and south forks of Long Island seem to be but two thin green rafts towed by invisible blue lines streaming farther out into the sea. It is a great, deep, and unpredictable body, the North Atlantic, whose bays—Shinnecock, Moriches, Flanders, Great and Little Peconic, Mecox, Southold, Noyack, and Gardiners (I am sure I have forgotten a few)—infiltrate our two peninsulas and make them even shallower masses, more responsive to sun and frost. If the spring is earlier on the north fork and the north side of the south fork, so too will winter be more extreme. The waters washing both forks give us a rather unruly spring, but they stay warm longer than an equal body of earth would, tempering the autumn and giving us a lengthy and lovely fall. Because of these cooling and warming differentials, both forks are windy places and both share in the salt the air carries. As a mitigant to all of this, true droughts here are rare, and dews are always heavy.

I plant in spring. I plant nearly everything in spring—shrubs, roses, berry bushes, hedges, pines, and evergreens as well as perennials. Nice as our autumns are, winter losses from driving winds are far too great to take the risk, unless I wish to apply antidesiccants and wrap trunks in tree wrap and bushes in burlap and generally spend much tiresome time cosseting. But here, except for spring-blooming bulbs and poppies and peonies and such, nothing should be planted in the autumn. I don't even chance grass or anything slower than a cover crop of annual rye, which sprouts in a matter of two or three days. A sad example of what happens is the rare and hardy rhododendron from mainland China I acquired last autumn, the only time it could arrive, which—although I took special pains in preparing its bed and welled up salt hay and burlap for protection and checked beneath to make certain the soil never dried out—looks quite awful. If its apical bud does not flush, I will have lost it. Another example: the one hundred box I lost last year, which I had lifted from the propagating bed to line the herb garden, the spot being a cove against the wind. No more tempting such fate. One can't plant against the season, and the season of peril out here is autumn, although it is a solid, traditional time for such moves elsewhere.

Our continual winds are so drying that I plant everything as if it were going into a hole in the middle of a desert, with double amounts of peat moss and a good broad sloping well to catch hose- or rainwater. Whatever the weather, whatever the rain, I follow a pattern of twice-weekly soakings, from an open hose whose end is tied in burlap to prevent the soil from washing away. And I stake anything that might rock in the wind and rip recuperating roots and fresh new ones before they can get hold. I don't care much for any of the recommended bulky things sold to stabilize a trunk to surrounding stakes, preferring strips of old shirts or sheets, those that I can spare from the studio. These are softer and just as sturdy, and although they are not as attractive, perhaps, by autumn they will have rotted and the savings will be large.

I prefer twilight for planting anything in leaf, the bed or hole being prepared during the day, which includes liberal soaking. It is an easy task to slip growing matter in and then give it an additional soaking; the coolness of the night and the morning dew will help the newcomer to recover. Although our last average killing frost date is April 23, many little freezes afterward can and do happen. Planting tender annuals and tender vegetable plants is very late out here. If you must follow the calendar, however, be advised that a night temperature of 50 degrees Fahrenheit or below may well be fatal to your stock. Wax-paper hot caps are a decent enough solution, if you remember to snip off the tops to avoid cooking the plants during the day. But they are also troublesome: earth must be piled on the edges lest they blow away. Having compared early planting under hot caps with late plantings without, I have seen little discernible difference in earliness of yield but much more vigor in plants that have not had to cope with a low thermometer during their infancy. A hot cap, remember, is a miniature greenhouse for only a few hours of retained daylight heat. It will carry a plant through a cold night after a shining day, but not if the day is cool and cloudy.

This leaves, of course, the wind factor throughout the spring and well into the early part of summer, when it tapers off a bit. I have found that an exposed vegetable garden is in much need of shielding, and I generally plant something on or near the rabbit wire around it. Scarlet runner beans are nice because the foliage is dense and the flowers are fine and you can get some beans from them, although more recent developments in beans are better than this nostalgic favorite. Morning glories are suitable. So, too, species clematis and the more robust roses. The rose need not be a rambler. A stout border of *Rosa rugosa* is an amiable hedge, liked by bees, who will then help pollinate and increase your bean, tomato, and squash crop, and the hips of these roses make fine fall jams and jellies. If you don't care for thorns, why not a wall of medium-sized sunflowers? Or a thicket of hollyhock. Or better still, enclose the entire patch in asparagus, whose plumes are thick, tall, and glorious.

Forecasters

A truly beastly March paces the path to spring and summer, gnawing at soil and bud, doing baton twirls with the thermometer, tossing clouds and the very air, bricking up the entrance to all that is green and wonderful with hail, frost, sleet, and snow blown from the portals of hell. It makes for dashed hopes, tests one's patience day and night. Like any border conflict it has an incendiary power. Precocious buds split under its attacks, and projects begun have to be halted.

When true and reliable warmth returns, it will make all endeavors more urgent. Will I have beds prepared for all the plants I have ordered? Get to prune the roses on time?

Yet this Rumpelstiltskin of a month would have indeed been forecast, but by two authorities I don't much admire, the *Farmer's Almanac* and the equally quaint U.S. Meteorological Service, both of which have often led me astray. With deplorable results. Despite all its weather satellites, the federal agency might just as well consider measuring the fat of bears as a more accurate indication of weather to come, for global warming is a fact they mostly ignore. It doesn't compute, is that it? But larger than that was that the recent birth of la Niña from el Niño (which does make one pause) gave them the greatest of outs. If it wasn't the one that made their computers spew ignorantly, it was surely the other. And two fall guys are better than one.

The *Farmer's Almanac* seems to work by averaging out weather phenomena, which is probably saner. When it comes to the inclement, moreover, it has a more elegant vocabulary. I'd much rather the almanac than the weather report. I have never felt so cold as I have since they invented wind chill. Thirty degrees and blowy is cold enough. To know that the wind chill is but three above zero is appalling. As for summer, dog days are dog days, and dogs know nothing of a temperature-humidity index. And then there are approaching weather fronts, but never backs. Cells of rain instead of buckets of same. News of weather alerts does not make my cat prick its ears or run under the sofa. Of course, Leopold is a rather odd cat, content to let Barnsley, the Norfolk terrier, do the reacting for him.

One's own observations are hardly any better. I find that seagulls come into the fields whenever the earth is turned and worms are abundant. A wildly exuberant storm keeps them at the shore, where they contentedly stare at their chests.

Red sky in the morning, sailors take warning? There is no naval base here, and I don't know any sailors.

Someone once told me that very fat mice in October were boilerplate indicators of a rough winter. My mice are incredibly fat all of the year.

And if there is an enormous crop of acorns? There will be many squirrels, and that is that.

When oak tree crimsons begin to show green is the time when you may safely set out the tomatoes. And have them rot.

The week after St. Patrick's Day is the time to plant peas and spinach. And their death shall be your reward, unless you think that caked shoes and muddied knees are a gift.

Until they decided to stay, migrating geese used to signal the advent of autumn's ending.

Spring is here, say the English, when you can crush seven daisies in one footstep. If you have size eighteens, this is possible. If you have size eighteens, stay out of the garden.

The list of old wives' and husbands' tales goes on and on and proves nothing more than that there will be weather. And plenty of it. As the late poet James Schuyler nobly stated, "I'm just glad there is some."

Foolish but optimistic gardeners like me go into their little greenhouses and start sowing.

Drought

If you read this and it is raining, or it has recently rained slowly and soakingly, with decent and thorough intent, you might defer these words until the Gobi visits you again. My sprinklers have been going full duty for over a month and I am tempted to cut the garden down. Beyond my mulching schedules and the practice of dense underplanting, all that lies between plant life and death is a tricky arrangement of quixotic sprinklers dampening the garden I have divvied into sectors. Oh, I have made the usual sanitations—plantings done with flowering are cut down, excess branches are clipped, and excessive bloomers are carefully disbudded, all helping to minimize evaporation and transpiration losses. I have even left invasive goldenrod around spring plantings of young shrubberies, the better to avoid water loss through soil disruption. And yes, we have had heavy nightly sea mists and ground fogs, and they have been of enormous help in this emergency, but not all leaves absorb wet this way. As the foliage is cleansed this way of field dust, we see by its browning that we are on red alert. We need prolonged rain.

Now sprinklers sprinkle, but then they gush. Or they halt in one position and drown in their own great inland seas. The pedestal ones, which I favor, for they go above tall specimens unimpeded, seem geared to soak the gardener in the slightest wind. Or they wind themselves right off their sticks and turn into municipal park drinking fountains. Although I hammer them into the ground with appropriately light and continuous taps, I find that they are not very strong and that they bend and then must be taken to a hard surface to be hammered straight again with what little patience remains. I used a soaker hose once but was not of a mind or disposition for a marsh garden in that particular spot. All of these gadgets are labor-heavy and bear constant watching, and none emulates the rain we desperately need, and none is as good as open trench warfare in the desert, where you place the hose in a ditch and watch the gracious stream pour through all the interconnecting canals.

If sprinklers cannot be made to work properly, I think

that hose manufacturers might partially compensate by making their products white. This green they favor, which is unlike anything that ever had roots, is nonetheless too perfect camouflage, perhaps because it is so ugly that the eye refuses to see it. I think of nice white hose lengths winding under white wicker furniture and across gray pebbles, down terra-cotta paths, and I like the idea. If the hose bleaches or discolors, so will the wicker chip and the pebbles get mossed and terra cotta fade, and probably in the same slow fashion. I wish too that all sprinklers came to us with small screen disks to keep whatnots from traveling to the sprinkler head and clogging them stationary. Some sprinklers have them, but not in pairs, and they are the first thing to go.

One of these errant machines contains a devil of a perverse performer. It is meant to swirl a full circle and then reverse direction. But what it does do is go half or three quarters and then reverse direction. In chugs. However I position it, it will not strike the planting I want it to. It goes over the hedge and waters my neighbor's towels. Or it recollects its 360-degree duties, but only when I approach from its seemingly "safe" side. Where it does water, it waters well, though.

The Indians of New Mexico placed chips of turquoise outside pueblo or hogan to bring rain. I must ask a friend if she brought any out when she moved here.

Gloria

Winter was balm for me that year. Its dark, empty hours rendered invisible the mutilations of Hurricane Gloria, some of whose brutishness became permanent and much of whose damages were not manifest until midspring or earliest summer. I feared that the earth might be piled then in dead stuff once more, just as it was in the late afternoon of September 27, 1985, when whether there was a garden under all that ripped green was not at all clear. There have been worse storms since I have been making Madoo, with higher winds and more flying salt, but those came at more appropriate, leafless times or much earlier in the growing season, leaving time for recovery before the year shut down. This storm was very late. It cut the electricity, so I could not work my pumps to sluice off the salt, which was so heavy my windows looked like mica. Browning went on throughout the evergreens like mold on shoes or foxing on a drawing. All herbaceous matter was mutilated. A stand of eleven Irish junipers was cut in half, each and every one. A copse of American cedars was dead on its seaward face. A young golden deodar lost its needles and an older one browned daily. It would be hard, next spring, to make of the wreck any symmetry or decent form; things were just too mangled, too torn.

The definite tree-toll was eleven, including a quite robust and elegant European larch which perfectly swept a short curved path, making it seem longer. When it came out of the chipper, the eighteen-footer made a surprisingly small pile, aromatic and green, the color of new pesto. And then it faded and reduced even further to underline the inescapable news that it was mostly air and tinted water. The sole remaining American dogwood went, the others having gone before from something viral. And the second willow I planted here, in 1967, leaving a hole of blue where sky pours in over mountain laurel and holly, far too bright for their cultivation. And two black pines. One of two cork-barked elms is now a stumpy, hideous thing, which sprouted back, of course, but gracelessly, as if it had been pollarded. Scald, or shall I call it singe or sea-burn, was all over a weeping white pine and a Nootka cypress. Flowers broke on the fruit trees and lilacs showed bits of bloom. The coming spring was a matter of bulbs, not bushes, and there were no apples, pears, or plums. One of the crab apples was in fruit and bloom at once. A rare and glorious *Franklinia* split all through its young trunk yet flowered, staked and taped, but how much salt had gone through to the phloem was unclear, and how much may have entered the root took next spring to answer. Its leaves fell faster than its petals, and all were brown. Autumn anemones had not begun their bloom or the cardinal flower finished in its flowering. All twenty feet of a wisteria were thrown from a wall but have been pegged back. The stiff runners scraped shingles blond. Brutal and nasty it all was, with not a pocket unscarred.

I wouldn't evacuate. The summer studio had been weathering storms since 1740. Town shelters didn't want dogs. The corgi hid in the dark paint racks, and neither aspirin nor petting consoled her. The Norfolk sat right before the door, growling at all the fuss. I saw a few favorite limbs bounding past, turned off the portable radio, and then took a nap on the shuddering floor. Crickets and birds were in full, even enlarged voice all through the short, pulsing winds, although I was told that a bit farther down the road, closer to the water, the only sound was wind and surf. Days later, huge colonies of monarch butterflies hung upside down on two black pines. One could touch them. I saw gaudy birds I didn't know the names of. And then the awful stench of rotting foliage thickened the air.

My phone was out for thirteen days, and the feeling was a little bit like being stone deaf and having the thought that someone was speaking but just too softly to hear. I forgot how to trim wicks properly and kerosene smoke got on everything and I began reading by candlelight or, early to bed, in a repeat of childhood wickedness, by flashlight. Tomato sauce I had put up was pitched along with the rest of the perishables. I made reacquaintance with the large and complicated world of canned foods. Washing in a small basin took time. I was back in a studio in Maine but with skills gone and no pump in the kitchen.

When the phone got on, the first call was from Rosemary Verey, at Barnsley House in Gloucestershire.

"I've been calling every day without getting through. I am sick with worry. Tell me how things are."

We went through the garden, tree by tree, bush by bush.

"Oh no. Not that nice dogwood. How dreadful. What will you do without the larch?"

It was a long, long call.

"I've thrown away my watch. I don't want to know how much this phone call will cost. And I do want to read you what I've just written on your garden and the storm for *Country Life* before I put it into an envelope. I mean, if you can do me in emeralds and eyeglasses for your paper, I don't see why I shouldn't have the same opportunity. But I did want you to pass on it. Now tell me—how are *you?*"

"Rosemary! I am so glad you asked. I thought you never would."

"Well, I am concerned."

"Simply said, Rosemary, I died."

"Of course."

Only by the next July did all the losses in the garden reach the end of the toll of casualty from the September hurricane. Only in those late days did the shadow of Gloria stop lengthening. Only then were all of the injuries in hand for fair dealing.

Throughout the spring of 1986, for example, strong laterals of the lopped cork-barked elm began to show more twig-death than seemed indicated. Because of their rude form and because their weakness would unnecessarily tap the maimed tree's central energy, I began removing them one by one, until only a single branch, fairly high up, full of promise, was left, in hopes of supplying a new leader. I was delighted to find, however, that robust sprouting began to occur all along the trunk, a habit of elms I thought this variety might not possess but happily did, so that I was able to remove the remaining length of the single lateral, leaving a stubborn-looking stub about twelve feet high, foaming with side issue, already giving hints of future shapeliness. As the new laterals progressed, I thinned them.

In the corner of the cork-barked elms, the wind hit hardest, a coved onslaught mercifully local, but two Russian olives, angling off from the elms, had to be skeletonized. Force remained in the limbs, yes, but in such random and erratic a fashion that it seemed better to lop and lop, reducing both specimens to a third of their original size, just as if they had been transplanted in some nursery, the better to develop more compact rootballs and denser shape. It took three years before the corner returned to decent form. I deflected the eye by brightening a pair of gates near the havoc in yellow and red and a strong blue mixed with rose, over which I strung clematis of the *davidiana* family. Behind one gate, 'Souvenir de la Malmaison' opened, and above it the *soulieana* rose was soon in bloom. A good cynosure, but I wished I could put up some woven straw fencing like the fine one the Pitti museum employs. The sign on it would read EXHIBITION BEING INSTALLED. I would keep the fencing there until things were less of a sight.

A long distance away, where the huge larch went down, destroying the counterpoint of two larches on either side of the path, touching, a medium-sized golden deodar suddenly snuffed out. It had begun to bud, and then the swelling stopped. I dug it up. Its taproot had been wrenched and two main horizontals snapped. How the tree had hung on so long I do not know. It had been maimed far too severely to throw out requisite restoring feeder roots. A touching, graceful tree. Its loss was painful.

Throughout the garden there were vibrant shrubs without good form, shrubs that I had pruned up and up through the years to achieve a light, fountaining effect. These had been made leafless by the storm. By late September and early October new growth had begun, and it never hardened properly before frost. All the tips were so studded with dead wood that I was forced to lop them (variegated weigela, white lilacs, variegated dogwood) straight off at the ground, where new and urgent issue pushed up. In those areas, too, woven palings would have been a nice idea, for the healing also took several years. Meantime, the gaps created strong absences, rather like a record skipping under a dusty needle, losing a bar or a whole phrase of melody.

All over, dead twigs continually fell. Raking them up was a weekly affair, an activity of the sort usually reserved for spring cleanup, twigs from heights beyond ladders or poles, twigs from dead trees and shrubs too numerous to attend to. Birches were dreadfully afflicted and looked broken and tatty and abused and forlorn and had to be left for the sort of pruning an average wind does, or the simplest urgings of sap against dead cells. I was more careful that season with deadheading rhododendrons and lilacs, for the vitality of these strong bloomers had to be sent into making leaf and branch rather than seed.

The following fall I mulched heavily and watered heavily before the garden went into winter. In spring, I fertilized more lavishly than I had been wont to. The result was a handsome, overall foliant effect. The larger view of the collection looked good, and lusty growth began blunting the effect of the scars. The lean had become full, the gone forgotten.

May

IF MAY IS the very heart of spring, it is also the opened eye of the preceding autumn. All of its major blooms were set at that time, and the generalized health and vigor and broad aspect of the garden is the manifestation of all the manuring and mulching undertaken during that season. The stance and stamina of each bush and tree are witness to the skill or the expertise of winter pruning.

May is half-foliage month, part architecture, part skin, the armature of all woody matter still visible under its immature coating of adolescent greens. Leaves vie with flowers—they are as fresh and as multicolored. Out of bud, bulb, and root they come in predominant reds and oranges opening in an imprecision of color adjustments swinging through all shades of fuzz, aureate like the moon's ring before rain, which is a color we cannot name. May expires in the eye quickly. No sooner is something visible than it is gone, either withered or worked into other energies.

Even without the usual showers, May looks fine in my garden; dryness doesn't affect anything except new transplants, which get misted as well as watered from sprinklers adjusted to their finest sprays. Morning and night. Years of manure and salt hay mulches keep all the remainder cool-rooted and steady in their feeding.

In February I cut an overly massive *Rosa glauca* right to its nubs with arc saw and shears, and the bush came on in May from the remaining stubs on fat new canes, packing the shrub into a more rounded, denser mass already looking fair. It will be fine by the end of June. The middle of this month should see it lower, arching again where before it had stiffened into a pinched ball, cumbersome and squat. A graceful shrub it will be, of strawberry-bronze leaves dusted over brown leathery greens, high in the eye whether in bloom or not.

Next to the rose a shagbark maple too young to illustrate its peeling has now been relieved of its juvenile staking, for it is already bent by the wind into a fine little tree that has lost that boring, cosseted nursery look and taken on an idiosyncratic growth plan more in keeping with what is around it. Two magnolias, for one, hybrids so lusty that they bloomed this May although but eighteen inches high, each with a great single cup. I have brought them forward from the meadow by the simple expedient of cutting the meadow grass back and away all around them, making them the final margins of a broad grass path that now stretches through fastigiate oaks, diamond-barked willows from the Great Plains, a grafted yellow elm, cledastrus, other magnolias, and shad—a path whose beginning is now a pair of blue gates.

I am getting to like the effect more and more. What I will add will depend on how the tall margin grasses I have put in will do. Blue specimens, variegated ones, all of which will bear and hold autumnal plumes that I think I will leave on their stalks through next winter. The entire mass will look, I hope, like a long, winding theme, notes with great spaces between them but rising here and there with bright accents, taking one to the end, but slowly, to the three pools where parts of the excursion will be reflected, just like a coda.

May is of course one of the busiest months, and I have put off the exasperating chore of transplanting leeks, for I have gotten used to large things and have no head for small. May is a month one can lose very easily if one does not do a task entire and forget proximate concerns. If one is transplanting columbine, one doesn't move woodruff simply because it is intermixed. Although it is the month of aggregates, each plant responds to it in its own way, with its own needs. Attention must be specific. It is not a month for a wandering mind.

Because the asparagus had been cropped heavily, I stopped its cutting, although I might have continued until the middle of June. Dwarf arctic willow I planted near its emerging feathers are close to the current of its blue tones. A fine company. I will see if santolina and medicinal rue will be appropriate, too. A single plant of each, moved from spot to spot, not planted but moved gently with plenty of rootball and studied each time from a distance. In May one adds and takes away, a bit at a time, working deliberately.

THE NAME OF THE ROSE

JUNE CAME LATE that year, almost at July, almost not at all. I thought they would never come, those June days all white and blue and warm, whose greens are still young enough to be blue and chartreuse; warm, fragrant days very much like the herald flowers of the month, roses. But the roses were very much on time that year, and because or in spite of the weather, they were larger, on longer canes and stronger stems, and they lasted longer than I have ever seen them last. 'Dawn' was fine and 'Coral Dawn' finer and 'Blanc Double de Coubert' and 'Souvenir de la Malmaison' and 'Nymphenburg'; all my roses were fine, including a fat bush rose called 'Garden Director Something Something Lindblatt' (if that isn't its last name, it is certainly something like it). There are three or four roses named after garden directors, and I have two.

As I imagine it, Herr Garden Director Lindblatt was at the point of retirement after a long, undoubtedly undistinguished reign as garden director of a small park somewhere in the middle of Europe, where his tenure had been politely, precisely custodial, and the park's plantings had remained as cozy as they had been when the previous head had stepped down. And now he too was stepping down. There were people in carriages and on horseback. There were swans and families strolling. There was the usual band in the vanilla-white bandstand. In the crowd were flower sellers. There was to be the ceremony of the rose. The margravine, alas, could not appear. She had not been well after the birth of her last child, but, kindness itself, she had sent a very important aide with a large coin struck in her image in a large purple velvet box. Her rule was a kind one. The realm, an enormous collection of little realms stuffed within a larger, looser one, each with its own uniform, flag, and musical salute, seemed, on the map of Europe, to resemble the large massed flowerbeds packed tight in intricate designs on the lawn, around which the citizens, like rivers, flowed. There was a very long speech, but everyone approved of long honorific speeches, and the ceremony of retirement is, after all, enormously important. At last the director made his speech, and it seemed to encompass all the others, flying higher and higher in its praise of ruler and kingdom and the good fortune that had been his. He was suitably humble. He had, after all, never changed a thing in the little park but had kept it neat, and it had flourished precisely as it had flourished under his predecessor, in imitation of the little kingdom where everything had been orderly and right for so very long. When the rose was presented to him and given his name, the garden director did something very extraordinary indeed. He gave it to his wife.

The history of roses is also the history of man. It is a history of his better side. Roses are named for generals but not for battles. For ladies who have touched the hearts of men, and if they were ladies who had touched the hearts of many men, they were ladies who also rose above liaison as a career and wrote or painted. Roses are named for moments mankind would like to fix in time. They remain the flowers of approval and applause. Because of this particularity, which has often been lost in time, their names are frequently very hard to remember.

I have a pale large yellow rambler on the potting shed wall. It reminds me of a climbing yellow rose I saw planted when I was three or four. My brother was planting it, watched by my mother, her sister, and my two cousins. Everyone was very quiet and I felt that quiet very clearly, for I did not know the reason for the stillness and the attention, yet I sensed that everyone else knew and that I was too young to know, and was enormously furious. The rose went into its hole and then the earth was shoveled in and then a can of water was given to my mother, who poured it, and then they all walked away and I still stood there until I was called. The rose I have today is probably not the same rose, and yet it seems to participate in the same quietness and the same relentless moment of it all. That I know the secret of that day now does not take away a certain fury from these yellow blooms, for the loss of a child is something no family can ever forget. My brother. His hair was yellow. He died before I was born, and the little ceremony had been for him on his birthday in June. It is often clear to me that my existence comes from his small body giving out in a fever. Another aunt once told me, "They were broken-hearted and decided to have another child."

I find it not at all strange that a large part of me is still close to Matthew Dash and that when I was ordering a rose for the potting shed, I went for a yellow rose, although yellow in roses is not at all the color I go for. I have forgotten its name. It has joined the collection I have, and after all, I think it should only continue the grand linking of the forms of life and dying, the sadness of it and its powerful perplexity and strange, unalterable joy, those many Junes man has turned to roses and planted them, naming them for fat garden directors, ladies true and ladies light, generals, wives, daughters, occasionally houses, sometimes friends.

Very probably the yellow rose planted over forty years ago in our garden in New York City has died. Eventually, so will this one I planted last year. Yellow is the color that goes into the ripening grain of the fields around me before it is cut.

Trees

THE LOVE OF TREES is pandemic. Even gatherers who wander the tundra or make their due near the great white ring around the pole or load deserts with their wanderings have in their legends tales of talking trees, forests of manna, husbanding trees, leafy dispensers of rest, shelter, and food. Every copse, spinney, or little wood has thus come to be emblematic of permanent settlement, water unbounding, unfailing fertility. Trees and grasses are resources ever renewable. Just as there is a great flood in the origin myths of all tribes, so too legends of trees fly throughout their rhythms as a dark raven does, immensely reassuring to the perplexed. Together with the smallest and earliest of the spring bulbs, trees are the most reassuring elements in the garden. Good gardens will always have young trees growing in them, somewhere, in a nursery, say, or in a section of the vegetable garden, or even dotted among flowers and bushes, until tall enough for more permanent installation. They mature or come to a fine shape sooner than is generally thought. I cannot imagine a garden without them, they and the smallest bulbs, for they trigger our most spiritual moments, the moments of obeisance and awe. As governments and religions know, looking down or up is something man does not usually do, and when he does his head gets lost (or is it clearer?) and is, at that moment, more available for being reached.

The youth of a tree is a pleasure to regard. It is also the most perfect time for molding it, adjusting it to the garden's needs, for making modifications in what it will eventually become. The most minor amendments (bending the main trunk or stiffening it, the removal or thinning out of superfluous side branches) will yield major changes in its ultimate frame and in far less time than one imagines, for trees in general invest in their greatest growth when they are young, in the first and second decades, a genetic recollection of the habitat of the forest and the crucial need to compete against others for light. For that reason it is imperative to plant saplings closely and thin them out later. A tree planted singly will grow fat, lazy, and leafy. If one wants the perfect specimen, there can be no better way than to jam in eight or nine evenly spaced in a small area and then select the most vigorous, destroying the rest. A good, clear bole is what one wants.

Nursery catalogues, so many of them, have hidden away somewhere offerings of rooted cuttings or two- or three-year-old liners, charges for which are modest. Or one can apply to specialist nurseries, which annually plant and distribute millions of replacements for our forests. Seeds too are offered by many firms.

PLANT PORTRAITS III

Wisteria

It produced the worst couplet I know of—"The crystal clear wistaria/After the storm's hysteria" (Edith Sitwell)—and fundamental English reticence founders before it. The *Dictionary of Gardening* of the Royal Horticultural Society describes it as "the noblest hardy climber ever produced." It is rare to find such an unrestricted encomium for anything at all in our gardens, be it those other royals the magnolia, say, and the lily, and comforting to find one's predilection for it finely endorsed. It has a large jarring moment in its history, though, one curious and provocative. It was named for Caspar Wistar, a professor of anatomy at the University of Pennsylvania (whose dates are 1761–1818), but then deliberately spelled *wisteria* by a Mr. Nuttall, the author of the genus, who thus named this glory for no one at all but retained enough of Wistar's name, of course, to deepen and underscore the hurt. Whatever happened between Wistar and Nuttall is lost in the many seasons of sun and shadow that have intervened. Wistar was one of the early owners of

Vernon Park, Philadelphia, and the vine that flourished there was probably one of the two species native to the eastern United States, not any of the four of eastern Asia. It is the *sinensis* (also known as Chinese kidney bean) that is the vine of our present gardens.

Wisteria attains great age, is thoroughly robust, and will do on nearly any soil, and yet it is—like all rampant, courageous plants—difficult to transplant except when very young and generally slow to take hold. But when it does, it is almost impossible to remove; I tried to rid the garden of one at the summer studio for years, and now, as the garden modified, it is more than acceptable and I have let it be. It can be had on the cheap, but one must beware of such bargains, for these are generally raised from seed and one may end with a lush, scrambling, flowerless vine, a seethe of green fodder. Because its roots are few but quite long, it is best to buy the plants in containers. Slip each one into a deep prepared hole, having gently loosened the long feeder roots so that they will voyage out and not in. (Container-grown plants very often develop a tropistic tendency to grow in the round after decanting, as if an admonition had been imprinted on the rootball, one never to be broken.) If one wishes to train wisteria into a small tree or bush with a single stem, it is rather easy to grow as a standard. After several years cut it back to a height of six or eight feet, whichever is most convenient, and pinch off side shoots along the stiffening stem until it is broad and rigid. At this time, if one keeps removing occasional side shoots, it will develop a gracious head or canopy and forget it has been a vine. It is a perfect weeper then, a more than acceptable substitute for weeping plum or cherry or even weeping crab. I could see a few such specimens dotted around a flat garden in a French effect of squares, with planked borders and pebbled paths. The fact that it takes to pruning so readily is often overlooked, and the general aspect of wisteria I see around me could very definitely use the knife. In Japan, its training will go along the edge of a house, horizontally along the eave line, with the vine annually cut back to spurs. In spring, leafage sprouts at the top of the vine while blooms hang pendant beneath.

There is white wisteria and blue, lilac and purplish, although the latter three colors are quite intermixed and blurred under cultivation and it is increasingly difficult to find true types. I grow a white, but it is smoked with lavender, and a blue with rose in it—or is it (as it sometimes seems) an abraded rose bruised, or a cold one? The flowers are like clusters of grapes made of flowering pea. They hold their color in wind and rain and they fall from their buddings as if mist were pouring from the darks of the vine. Late spring is their time from spurs, and they often bloom in autumn too, from the tips of terminal shoots. The entire mass will look venerable before not too many years have passed. Replacements are hardly ever needed, but additions can be made by the simple business of layering a shoot or two and detaching it from the main stem the following year.

If you wish wisteria in alleys, I would mix it with laburnum. Wisteria is lovely up a tree. I would select one a bit gaunt in its lower parts and allow the vine to climb the forty or more feet it will go, where tree and vine will live symbiotically, host and guest, with no restriction to either. If I had a gully, I would let one go up and down it. Old farms whose arbors have crashed frequently have them flat on the ground, but rearing up in waves and loops like the outlines of whitecaps, the old stems providing armature for the new. They are perfect overhangs at windows, but when thick, the ruin of shingles. Simple annual sanitary pruning should remedy that, however, and a trellis is superfluous. A peg on a wall is enough—the vine will do the rest. If your entrance looks hard, wisteria will soften it.

I would avoid the double form as an embellishment on the purity of the flower not at all called for. It is, moreover, not as prolific in its blooms. There is a variegated form, however, I think I would like to have.

Clematis

As I find increasingly appropriate situations for them, I also find that I keep adding to my holdings of clematis, and I now have more than four dozen plants, many of which I have raised from seed. In two cases beautifully thriving vines were simple volunteers. This is all quite nice, for clematis has rather unfairly been put down as a weak or problematic performer. Gardeners often think twice before acquiring one and then plant it fussily, even leerily. Such tentative attitudes and techniques can only increase its rather simple problems. Beyond its fondness for lime and need for cool roots and a hot top, average rich loamy garden soil will do for it. Infrequently it comes down with this terrible wilt, generally in midspring or any time when it is growing well. In the morning, the leaves and shoots will suddenly droop from stem tip to base; by the time the day is over, the plant, for all purposes, is quite dead. We don't know why and there is no cure and virtually nothing is known of the disease. The only thing to try is pruning the plant right to the ground and removing all fallen foliage. Like as not, the plant returns, rejuvenated, if not, not.

Delphiniums are far trickier and have a way of vanishing from their plantings. Roses make demands all through the year and come down with just about everything. Trouble is the middle name of phlox in July and August. Yet the clematis is stuck with the reputation of being wimpy. Pity. By growing many of them, one can incorporate possible loss into the general garden plan and the failure of a few will not be disastrous, which is one reason I grow so many. I have as yet not lost any, but I am prepared to. My surmounting reason, however, is that they are lovely and obliging and perfectly enter into the most experimental sorts of garden schemes. I grow only a few on trellises. The rest go up shrubs, which is the way they go at their lives in the wild.

If you must grow them on trellises, the webbing must be very tight indeed, for the bark can crack easily. Wind, even a small blow, sifting through a sagging trellis can cause much damage. They like leaf mold and manure, and if you can't shade their roots with a rock, then plant some low things around the base; dwarf rhododendron is not too bad an idea, as it is a noninterfering surface feeder. Florida hybrids and *patens* hybrids flower on old wood in spring and new shoots in summer and should not be pruned until after spring bloom. The 'Jackmanii' hybrids blossom on new growth and may be pruned in early spring.

Clematis is a genus of some 230 species of herbaceous, semiwoody, and woody climbing plants of the temperate regions of both hemispheres but chiefly the northern. One of their fascinations is that the leaves sometimes support the vines by curling their stems around supporting devices such as thin twigs or even dry stalks of some ghost of a plant. The Greeks, however, seem to have been generally unimpressed with them, and their name comes from *klema*, meaning vine-twig. They left it at that, which is rather an odd thing to do to such an innately interesting vine. But others have paid it greater heed, and we find a cluster of names for it in France and England and Italy: virgin's bower, gray beard, old man's beard, traveler's joy, grandfather's whiskers, Father Time, hedge feathers (that's nice), and snow-in-harvest (better still). French beggars rubbed freshly crushed leaves on their skin to cause sores and ulcers, and this is possibly why, in the language of flowers, clematis is the symbol of artifice and falseness. In some Anglo-Saxon countries sections about pencil size of the dry, woody stems of *Clematis vitalba* were cut into small bits and smoked, so that it also had the name of smoking cane or shepherd's delight (even though I always assumed that sheep were the true delight of the shepherd). Generally speaking, the smaller the bloom, the greater the scent, and it hits like the hawthorn, with vanilla or nutmeg thrown in for general headiness and whelm. As far as growing clematis from seed, hybrids will not breed true but species do.

During the nineteenth century, a Mr. George Jackmann began hybridizing them, and their popularity grew to such an extent that by the time he had published his grand monograph, "The Clematis as a Garden Flower," one could find gardens where only clematis grew. I imagine the gardens to have been very nice indeed, a bit foamy and moundy, a garden of cushions rather than plant furniture, but this would depend on the type of support used, I suppose.

The first specimen I grew from seed was *Clematis recta*,

which is really only half upright. Although it can take care of itself without staking, it is a bit of a flopper and consequently uses a lot of room, but this is fine because its foliage is a modest but attractive blue. It seeds a lot, and so does the yellow *tangutica*, which entered Kew from St. Petersburg in 1898. Sweet autumn clematis—*paniculata*, then *maximowicziana*, now *terniflora*—came from Japan and does fabulously throughout the Northeast. I have mine over yew for autumn brightness, and I think I will try this on silver birch next year. The 'Duchess of Edinburgh' is the finest white double but gets a bit frowzy in the summer heat, when its leaves seem to sizzle and fry dry brown. Behind the Duchess I have a species with the tiniest nodding amethyst blooms threaded through an old broom, alleviating its summer dullness with these violet, violet-blue marks that are at first hard to see, but then you do. I would like to try some especially vigorous clematis flat on the ground, and I think I would work it so the vine got pegged down at intervals in order to roam and maintain a large, robust shape. I might do this near some high-branched tree, whose mild, mottled light would probably be kinder than a full day's exposure to sun. All of mine get sun for half a day.

Last year I planted a new hybrid with *davidiana* in its ancestry. A pale blue fellow, it took the season to take hold and has performed magnificently this year. I settled it on an old barnyard gate I painted pale blue—or is the color a kind of white that blues with age? I am not entirely certain, but I believe that the plant's name is 'Robert Brydon' or 'Mrs. Alfred Brydon', and I do most certainly recommend it. (I know that I should tag or label my plants, and once I started to, with an enormous box of nice little aluminum tags one embossed on site with a nail or a pencil and then affixed to the specimen with a thin dark wire. But however inconspicuously I placed them, I began to feel that the garden was dogtagged. Little motions of the air got them wobbling and winking through all the green. So I stopped.)

Do grow clematis. Did I say that the ancient Romans had them on their house walls because they thought the vines gave protection against thunderstorms, and that the old Germans thought the reverse, that they attracted lightning and thunder? Or that it is reported that one can cook the very young shoots of *Clematis vitalba* and that the dish is said to be good? I do sometimes think of salads of daylily buds, fern fronds, and milkweed shoots, or are the possibilities so large and obvious that it might just be anything young and greening?

The Man with a Spade

Turning the soil of the vegetable garden in leafless air neither warm nor quiet, muscles in slow but heavy play, a man with a spade remains the supreme image of the agriculturist, and this task of turning is for me the most deeply satisfying act of the growing year. To do a thing so little changed in gesture and intention. With stick or finger, early man poked a hole for a seed, and what we do now is not very different. The wire against rabbits is the same principle as his fence of wattles. The hilling of the earth for irrigation rills is similar to his cupped hands full of water. Our welded steel blades bolted to wooden handles cultivate the same way his bones or stones tied to lopped saplings with leather strips or wythes did. Growing food for the table is so plain, so logical.

Very much older ways of cultivation are returning. The raised bed instead of rows. Double digging. Whether or not they will remain part of our contemporary gardening vocabulary will be up to the gardener's patience, for one, his strength, for another, and for a third his ability to adapt both to today's garden requirements.

Organic gardeners, who like to maintain that their principles are too "natural" ever to change, were very much against double digging at first, or for that matter, real digging at all, believing it to be interruptive of the natural capillary action of the soil. They built their soils much like forest or hedgerow, layering up organic matter year after year, and in that slightly loosened rotted duff would plant their seeds. It was no good at all to remind them that a vegetable garden is hardly natural. No part of the garden ever receives so many alien species or is so continually cropped and replaced. It seems now that they have gotten around this by bringing up the fact of impaction resulting from walking on the soil, and I would like to bring up that this same fact of impaction happens quite naturally from the ordinary settling of the same soil. Impaction will create a kind of subsoil hardpan, or erosion from underneath, if you will, which, rich or not, will stop moisture flow and keep nutrients locked from the root. This doesn't happen in the forest because the root of a seedling oak is adapted to such struggle, but that of our lettuce is not, which is why we were digging and loosening the soil in the first place.

So I will continue my double digging, having never stopped. Slowly. A back-weary and leg-sore gardener is of no use for days. What I will do afterward, however, is make more beds and raise them this year, for it does make a lot of sense and I have been doing this a little bit but ought to do it a lot. I first saw raised beds in the yard of our neighbor's house in Washington Square as a child. Beds raised above paths, beds narrow enough to be cultivated without a hoe, beds never walked on, where lettuces and basils and garlic and onion all grew together in the spring. In summer, each had a single tomato vine, usually staked but sometimes not, with quick leafy crops somehow stuck here and there, basking in the tomato vine's shade, for they were vegetables that needed shielding from the hot days of summer. Companion crops. And sometimes flowers were mixed in too. Mainly, however, vegetables, and no part of the soil was ever without plant cover, and things went in and out and made marvelous patterns as they did. It was like a medieval physick or herb garden, or one of those wonderful gardens in great tapestries where minstrels play within the wall, milady sits reading, and dogs they leap and leap. They had dogs. And cats. The grandfather was a violinist. All they lacked was a unicorn.

Raised beds can be of earthen sloped sides or enclosed in wood or stone, and the paths can be of straw or stone. It is up to you. Vegetables are planted at equal distances, not in rows, but with an idea of ultimate growing posture, lettuces six inches every which way but in their early stages closer than that, for you will be pulling them for the bowl and you may then dot the spaces with onion and garlic. Generally speaking, a root crop is always compatible with a top crop, their feeding habits being different enough not to crowd one another. Herbs can go in with the vegetables. The eye should be consulted in all of this, for these beds can be quite lovely. The rubiness of beet stem with lettuce, for example.

As far as quantity goes, the bed system, properly employed, should equal and surpass that of the row, for each plant is tended like a prize, and each will grow to specimen size and quality.

Mother

Someday they will discover the DNA of gardeners, for it is often inherited. My green thumb comes from Mother. Up until the very last day in the apartment she had for fifty-two years, Mother was striking cuttings, willing things to grow. I knew that her stay was ending when her plants began dying, her energy, will, and eyesight failing. A new collection is beginning on her windowsill out here. Mostly the nurses tend them, but her genetic fuse is still firing away. "How is the garden? I can't wait to see it." And she will, from a perch in the black wheelbarrow I or Carlos will handle. "Do you still have the azalea?" And I recall how furious I was with her for bringing it, a poor little wilted Mother's Day offering she had found next to the freight elevator, still in its silver foil and ghastly bow. "I'm sure it's one of those gaudy hybrids! But it will die if you don't plant it." To let anything green fail is a large, unpleasant sin. In it went, and it wasn't, wasn't the bawd I thought but a quite wonderful delicate native swamp variety. A good pale pink on layered branches with presence and heft.

Mother brought me dwarf boxwood for my first garden and a bundle of my earliest garden tools. I remember how she gravely cut in four my first radish, a quite miserable specimen, as I recall, placed it as the centerpiece salad, and pronounced it better than any radish she had ever eaten. I remember weekend trips to the lake place and the many stops we made en route at nurseries, the car getting forested. We used to go berrying, and we combed the hills for wild grapes she made into jams, even the green bunches I brought her. I would interrupt her, whatever the occasion, chatting on the phone, having tea with a friend: "The roses are out!" or "The partridge has berries."

Yet she did have an odd, rather ruthless side. Any bush that shadowed the chair she read in, she chopped to the ground. Anywhere she put her chair had to be permanently sunny. When it became shady, she went on the attack.

She viewed all containers as possible pots for plants, be they porcelain, china, glass, or tin, cracked or whole. A washing pitcher and bowl turned into a mass of arrow vine. A chamberpot ended up a thicket of cyclamen.

She is my earliest garden memory. I see her in white dress, white hat, white gloves, bending over German iris, cutting back fans, searching for grubs.

"I never gardened in white. However, if it's your image of me, run with it."

Arthur McCullough and His Willow Water

Willow water is catching on. It has been analyzed and come out with high marks, but the ghost of Arthur McCullough, a pitifully bent wizard of a nurseryman-gardener I knew when I was nine, would never be the sort of uneasy specter to need vindication. The second son of a gardener, whose father had been a gardener first in Scotland and then near London, where he "did" townhouses, Arthur was the most practical poker of the soil I ever knew and did not believe in superstition. Arthur knew what worked and what sometimes worked and what had never worked. Green lore came out of him like leaves, and like a sparrow I picked up on Arthur, whatever he did. Willow water, for one.

You take an end shoot of a willow tree, preferably one with vital young branches, and you lop it on a slant ("go for the juices") and you chop up the whole thing (or if you have time, you strip the bark and use that alone) and drop the mass in a pail of water to steep. Old wisdom recommends two to four days' retting, but Arthur's pail of mixing steeped for a week before the whole gummed mass was drained out; the liquid was then used to root cuttings in. Two to four days they say now for the cuttings, but Arthur's stayed in the stew for a week. He then followed normal procedures for rooting. In they went in the propagating bed, which was shielded from direct sun by laths, and that was that. Now we are told to dip the cutting tips after their soaking in any one of a number of hormone preparations available in nurseries and hardware stores. They still don't trust Arthur. I do, but I go him one better, for I dilute the willow water and wet down the cutting bed with it. I think he might have approved.

Bent Arthur, bitter Arthur, muttering Arthur, a sad fingernail-paring of a childless man attached to a trowel and a pair of shears, knew all about how willow wythes infuse clear water with their stupendous ability to send out roots no matter how dry, no matter how indifferently stuck in the earth. Isn't the story of the weeping willow's advent in England to do with a woven basket of dried Smyrna figs? How the king, on hearing about the beauty of the tree the basket came from, ordered it to be planted, whereupon it tossed out white rootlets, as is its wont, and prospered extremely? Wise old king. I would have planted a fig. But I suppose willows would have come anyway. The old worn-out basket would have ended most likely somewhere in the trash, if it hadn't been tossed on the fire, and the same thing would have happened. I think it just had to. England is made for willows.

On his limited means (he had a small pension from the

railroad for his broken back), Arthur used willow water to increase his specimens and make a nursery in record time. Arthur's secrets became mine, because I think he knew we were kindred trolls, entirely convinced that the properties of plants could be transferred if one only knew how. A variant form of the old doctrine of signatures, I guess, in which whatever is shaped like the organ that ails you has power to cure it, whether it be in the leaf of it or the root or the bud or the blossom; there it is, somewhere, waiting to get out. And so you pounded or you dried or you boiled or you stewed or . . .

I do hope Arthur McCullough would be pleased with my garden, whatever form he's in now, but it still might be hard to tell. He took success and failure like the sour realist he was. "Eggs today, feather dusters tomorrow": Arthur in a nutshell. I can't imagine why he had a skinny nine-year-old around, except that I mostly didn't ask questions and I did help him a bit as I shadowed him. Arthur was as accepting of my presence as of my absence. I'd be there every day for weeks. And then not.

His nursery and garden were on a narrow macadam road on the Orange and Rockland county border, on a hill no one knew what to do with. So they sold it to Arthur. A hill of trash boulders and enormous copperheads weltering in poison ivy, bittersweet, and Virginia creeper. Arthur planted all in soil dug from the woods around—native wildlings and then, when he had more money, whatever rare and beautiful things he liked. Willow water was his secret way of multiplying them in order to sell them and support his peculiar, wonderful ways. Three glorious acres.

What is there now is a wider highway. His garden would have made the road bend a bit, and they wanted it straight.

Ainsworth Cyphers

One of the greatest gardeners I have ever known about (or heard of) never gardened. His name was Ainsworth Cyphers, and he shot himself. My father hired him when no one else would, and I don't know why no one hired him, but I do know my father did. He worked. He was the most unremitting of men when he had a pickax and the most difficult when he had no tool in his hands. He labored on our slope, clearing trees with perfect eyes for how the light would come through older trees, which then flourished. He stooped for the partridgeberry and wintergreen and somehow knew where a colony of lady's slippers would come back. He took tree-sized rhododendrons from the swamps near Wanaque and planted them on our hill.

I have just been rereading Frank Kingdom Ward's last compendium of travels through Sikkim and Nepal and Tibet, and the illustrations of some rhododendrons sighted above peaks and rain-forest growths can be equaled only by the eye of Mr. Cyphers going through the northern New Jersey marshes, looking up, sighting these specimens, and somehow digging them out, toting them out of these peculiar tropics, and planting them, and they all survived. I think he was just indifferent to them. As a child I watched him plant them. He had a maximum of courtesy to the hole and a great belief in the ability of woodland thieving to survive. He never staked them and he never watered them and he never topped the ground with duff. As all the great gardeners do, he never cared about the look of things when he had done with them. Painters too are like this.

When I was eight, Mr. Cyphers somewhat adopted me and took me on long walks through the old Sterling Forest lands, where during the Revolutionary War mining went on. He showed me pits where charcoal had been made. He showed me springs hidden under mountain laurel, where usually one wise frog would monitor bugs. He took me once to a farm that had been abandoned before the Revolution and showed me outlines of the foundations and lilacs blooming next to them. He showed me the old orchard, and it was here that he gardened. For the deer. He kept all the apple trees (he called them *dusticoat*) trimmed and healthy, his only tool a hatchet. Why he took me on all these long walks, I still don't know. I think it was a gift to my father. I also think it was because he knew I liked them. We walked in silence. It was at this farm that Mr. Cyphers shot himself. My father always paid him in cash. Mr. Cyphers could not endorse checks. He was illiterate.

Gertrude Jekyll

The little book in its persimmon jacket lay on the dinner table, next my notebook, next morning coffee, salad tossed for lunch, seared chicken for dinner. And the whole of the next day's diet too, frequently joined by the cat, who disgustedly found it not large enough for a nap. Occasional berries from a sprig of Russian olive fell on it as well as food.

A most messy life, I fear. My domestic scene is that I cannot eat without reading, or read without smoking. But not one without censure, for during Thanksgiving my stolen reading got spotty swipes from a stream of guests:

"I can't believe you're still reading her."

"Can't bear that woman."

"Can't you see how irrelevant she's become?"

And such-like.

Poor thing. Poor book. Poor Aunt Bumps (the nickname Ned Lutyens bestowed on her in a letter). *Colour in the Flower Garden* is in a new edition from the Royal Horticultural Society's Classic Garden Writers series. The author, of course, is Gertrude Jekyll (like Hyde's fellow, pronounced "Gee-kull").

I tried to explain that there is much to be had from everyone and anyone who ever took pains to write on gardening and that I frequently turn to Theophrastus and Varro and Virgil as well as distinctly modern masters—Elizabeth Lawrence, Rosemary Verey, Mirabel Osler, Penelope Hobhouse, Vita Sackville-West (but oh, not that awful long poem), Anne Raver, Christopher Lloyd, Reginald Farrer . . .

It is not the dear old thing's fault that she got such smarmy, gushy press. It is not her fault either that she was swallowed whole for about a decade when all things English were the rage. I recall my eyeballs getting frocked silly with Laura Ashley, while relentless bowls of potpourri deadened my nose. Walls of dismal rural watercolors, paintings of loyal dogs, and huger ones of horses, hunts, and thatched cottages swirl in my memory. I knew someone who made a collection of Huntley and Palmer commemorative biscuit boxes. It was a period when, it seems, all of America was out to tea, or dipping chintz into it to get that *de rigueur* fade.

Of course, no one ever quite got the "English country look," which is a jumble of vetted antiques mixed with repros, broken legs and arms here and there, good paintings jammed against atrocious ones, untuned pianos swathed in shawls and staggering under photographs, no central heat-ing, lots of puppies and hounds, and an occasional visiting horse. Damp spots on the wall.

We began to have English borders and all-white gardens. Vintage wellheads and blurry stone cupids with arrows gone. No pond was without a swan. Poor Miss Jekyll became a part of all of this Burberrying, a sort of Florence Nightingale in the Yalta years of American gardening, when colonial inferiorities bounced back again, masquerading as good form.

And then we knifed her, the poor, undeserving soul, when we found that a good English border had to be at least 20 feet wide and 300 yards long, backed by a 15-foot-high wall of golden Cotswold stone. We discovered that we were a continent and not an island, had heat waves and droughts and violent winds and frosts three feet deep. Out she went, and with her, her many well-written wisdoms:

> All gardening involves constant change. It is even more so in woodland.
>
> Good gardening means patience and dogged determination. There must be many failures and losses, but by always pushing on there will also be the reward of success. Those who do not know are apt to think that hardy flower gardening of the best kind is easy. It is not easy at all. It has taken me half a lifetime merely to find out what is best, worth doing, and a good slice out of another half to puzzle out the ways of doing it.
>
> Even a proficiency in some branch of fine art does not necessarily imply ability to lay out ground. I have known, in the intimate association of half a lifetime, a landscape painter whose interpretation of natural beauty was of the most refined and poetical quality, and who truly loved flowers and beautiful vegetation, but who was quite incapable of personally arranging a garden.

The above and much more are all from this tiny book of 160 pages. There's scarcely one I haven't made a check on, and whole paragraphs have exclamation points next to them. That she did make her gardens for a time when purses were bulging and labor was cheap doesn't make her irrelevant. She also designed a windowbox for a little boy in the Midlands. The plan is in one of her books.

Roses

JUNE IS, of course, the most beautiful month in the garden. Everything major and wonderful seems to be in bloom, and the roses in my garden and the roses in yours—the wild white dog roses in the hedgerows and the nameless red roses on countless locust post railings—all are heralding the season to come. "Summer's long road," wrote the poet James Schuyler, "lined with roses and thunder."

One of my favorites is a chaste pink sparkler packed with over a hundred petals from the empress Josephine Bonaparte's garden, Malmaison. Josephine's catastrophic dressmakers' bills are well known, but she spent more, much more, on her gardens at Malmaison, from whose cutting and propagating beds went thousands of plants and shrubs to gardens royal and plain throughout Europe. A highly extravagant Johnny Appleseed, she was in the front ranks of the obsessed amateur in her green zeal, and the French treasury was nearly bankrupted as the earth of Malmaison was planted, dug, and planted, over and over again. We are all in her debt. Although she never neglected her floral alphabet, roses were her favorites. She carried one cupped in her hand and, it is rumored, held it to her lips, the better to hide her very bad teeth when she spoke, in a voice described as hoarse, low, and rapid. Embroidered in the marbles of her dining room floor was a small rose, and on it her chair stood. On a certain late morning, a Russian nobleman was taking his leave and received from her lips and hands a rose without a name. With prompt and courtly diplomacy, he said, "Madame, I will call it . . . 'Souvenir de la Malmaison'." The rose of leave-taking.

It is a magnificent rose, pink—the pink we call the cheeks of Renoir children, although they are red. It is a leaping trout pink, this rose. And the petal power of the four-inch flowers stuccoed along extremely well arched stems, loaded to the ground, will cover a wide area and leave you a bit short of breath when they're all out and just beginning to scatter. Let them; don't sweep them up, for they go into a nice musty linen color when they dry and are equally fine. 'Souvenir de la Malmaison' is complaisant and generous enough to be a remontant rose, blooming with less enthusiasm but great constancy throughout the growing season. Because it is a Bourbon rose with more than a little China tea in its background, it is a bit weak and is not considered reliably hardy in our area, but here is a way to get around this. Peg the stems down wherever they touch the earth. Make a tweezer by splitting a garden bamboo stake, or if you have a nice rock, then a bit of earth and the rock on top will do. During the growing season, the canes will strike root. Should winter kill the host plant, one or two of these will remain quick and will flower true and you will be able to continue enjoying Josephine's *nuit d'amour*. A constant, undisturbed mulch of salt hay placed each autumn around and under the main plant, decently manured on top, will be all the winter preparation and major nutrition it will require.

For all of its excellent floral vigor and fine shape (like a green fountain, collapsing), 'Souvenir de la Malmaison' should relate to the whole scheme of your garden and never be placed in a spot of undue prominence. That it is a rose and that we all love roses does not mean that roses are not, somehow, flowers. We do not want to see them all the time, nor do they have enough reliable architectural form to pose in the front position of the border. As with all gross and vigorous feeders, roses are in need of constant pruning and, owing to their complicated, overbred inheritance, afflicted with many deplorable moments. Roses are always coming down with something. I don't spray and you mustn't spray. In our part of the world, everything put on top of the earth quickly enters our drinking water. Unchanged. And I don't believe in those recipes filched from some mythical granny's apron pockets, composed mostly of garlic and hot pepper. They belong in salads, not in the rose garden.

Since the appetite for roses is never satisfied, I continue to plant and experiment with different varieties, hoping to enlarge my collection, unable to resist ones that promise miracles (and give nothing of the sort). 'Nevada', for example, is so splendid, with large, almost mallow-size blooms, yet never stays over a winter for me (although it is generally considered "reliably" hardy). The green rose I don't grow any longer, really a miserable little freak, not at all worth the effort and really green only under specific cloudy light, with proper background as a foil. The 'China Monthly' I do continue to grow, for it is the rose that blooms into

December and ought to be called the first rose of winter rather than the last rose of summer. 'China Monthly' is also the first rose to get sick. But the great majority of roses are so much disposable, overly celebrated, highly undependable, foolish junk and ought never to be planted in the garden. Or sold, for that matter. Through the years, with a mountainous amount of labor and an embarrassing outlay of cash, I have assembled a moderately reliable core, a unit of good fellows, and if I had a nursery these are the only ones I would stock.

The pillar rose, as I believe the term should be understood, is the sort of rambler that is of stouter stem and less randy growth, entirely adapted to running around a vertical support, a rose of medium to long growing length. On a twelve-foot post I have 'Dortmund', a Kordes development. It blooms all the time, although sometimes a bit less so, a diminished interval of performance the reason for which I don't understand. Crimson red blooms whose eyes are white. Single-petaled. In great clusters never topped by wind, whose fallen petals leave a mass of vigorous hips good for winter flower arrangements when they turn this wonderfully shiny mahogany. Because its canes are robust, it is not the easiest rose to twine, and one has to wait for a good long length before twisting it in the conformation one wishes. The base of 'Dortmund' often will spray out with perfectly reliable, nondepleting small shoots. These can be left if one is after that sort of cushioned effect or if the post is isolated and can be seen in the whole round. Otherwise, out they go, with some regrets, for it is a nice effect, generous with the dark foliage that gives 'Dortmund' its especial snap, foliage untouched by disease and never marred by age. Old foliage is as good as new, just as glossed up at the end of the season. The stems, too, unless three or more years old, are a most attractive crisp lettucelike color.

'Dortmund' could do with breeding down. I think it might also make a nice bush rose. It is a medium to heavy feeder, but it is quite calm when getting little. When this occurs, it is more parsimonious with its blooms, while it shoots more, as if seeking nourishment. Should one forget to deadhead it, flowering will be as frequent but with fewer blossoms, so 'Dortmund' is a wonderful rose for a neglectful gardener, being one of those specimens so much always there, doing its duty, that one comes to observe it less and less and lapses of care are often its reward. It is, however, a rose to concentrate on, and I have painted it once in reverse, a small canvas of it as a white flower with a red eye, thinking all the time that a variety of that sort might not be an improvement, no, but such a splendid amplification that I would then put in another post at the other end of the long path, and then I think I would find 'Dortmund' difficult to ignore.

White is composed of all colors, and white flowers tend to waver back into faded memories of their components, no longer true, a blurry thing in the background of an old snapshot becoming curiously defined, almost prominent. White flowers readily go bone in the sun, or tin, or a pale tin running tan, or go gray generally suffused with pink. Each year I plant so-called white Italian sunflowers and they are really pale yellow, but then, I remember, so is macaroni on the plate but rarely in its illustration on the box, and white Italian sunflowers are white only in the photograph on the seed package, as white as the white of white roses shining in catalogues of roses. I cannot recall how many white roses I have planted and tried against blue cypress, gray shingle, black-green yew, and all have been pasta yellow, pretty close to flour mixed with egg. They open in the morning already looking old.

All, that is, except the tissue-paper rugosa rose 'Blanc Double de Coubert', not cream, not skimmed milk, but rain-free cumulus-cloud white, always suggesting a clear, clear day. It is so notably free of fugitive tint that it will darken surrounding foliage and not the other way round, or make surrounding leaves seem fresher. And though its own foliage has undiminished, ingratiating freshness, going from apple green when young to almost mature apple when older and then, in autumn, to the most brilliant high ocher, the flowers are always the superior color of the finest white bond.

You must plant it. I am thinking of extending its domain here to a meadow garden I am considering making. And just about everywhere else. I imagine planting it in drifts. Near it, in a second little meadow garden I dream of, I will plant 'Fru Dagmar Hastrup', a pink rugosa rose.

Before I plant I will stalk the rhythm of the place, particularly the fall of shadows through the uneven ground. I can't imagine a meadow garden on the flat. I will plant these two rugosas exactly like shadows, to consolidate further the feeling of random distribution. 'Blanc Double de Coubert' especially. It is such a cynosure that it otherwise could overwhelm the two compositions. I think it might, however, be planted as a hedge breaking away, and this would be a fine idea for a limited space—a strict row broken, a falling-out of a pattern, as if the roses had self-sown.

Rosa soulieana is one other member of my core group.

Redoubtable ramper that it is, I use it as a groundcover on a small hill, but its fruits are better than its blooms, the former lasting all winter and the latter for only a week or so in June, as wild and wonderful as the wild dog rose, whose flower it most resembles. It too could be part of a meadow garden, as very definitely could the Scotch briar rose, as unembarrassed a suckerer as ever grew, one I would relegate to a patch one never thinks of entering. We do need more bush or park roses for such tricky situations, and old ones are indeed being revived and new ones developed at Iowa State University. Griffith Buck developed 'Applejack', whose foliage smells of apple and whose frank pink blooms go on through the season to such an extent that its figuration seems permanently pink. An area with it in uninterrupted performance could get a bit tiresome, rather like a whippoorwill, refreshing at first and then definitely pure "Chopsticks." I wouldn't plant 'Applejack' in a small space, where variety is at a premium. It gets bigger year after year, and should be allowed to do so, young branches resting on old. Although I have many other roses—*Rosa glauca*, 'Madame Alfred Carrière', 'New Dawn', 'Coral Dawn', 'Lawrence Johnston', 'Cornelia', 'Climbing American Beauty', 'Austrian Copper', *Rosa roxburghii;* the list is very long—I find that I can't recommend them in full heart. Beyond the few exceptions I have already mentioned, I must beg attention to any and all rugosas. They are far and away the best bet for the gardener short on time and high in eagerness to find varieties able to take wild indispositions of weather. Rugosas are the only positive answer, rugosas brusque and good-looking, heavy on prickles. Bees love the flowers, and birds their berries. Picked, they last. Planted, they last. They are to the seacoast bred and will take sandy soil and salt air and dryness at the root, or even considerable damp. I am making a hedge of quite a few varieties, the sort of hedge one sees in one's mind billowing low to high, straight up and bending. I look forward to a large bench in front of them. A good place to talk, the rose being the flower of confession.

Paths

Doing nothing but hanging about and musing or letting one's feelings roam is also what a gardener is all about. All good garden paths should lead to loitering with fine intent, and if they don't, then something is wrong indeed. Loitering is horticulturally permissible behavior. A garden is sculpture in the round, and except for a main utilitarian thoroughfare wide enough for a wheelbarrow, all guides to the foot should be slowed passages past the display, the better to lengthen expectation and build surprise. If they aim you away from the house, you are on the right track. If none of them is permanent (a garden path should adjust to growth and not restrict it), you are more than halfway home. Ending up where you hadn't planned to is basic to the charm, which is what Emily Dickinson had in mind when she wrote, "Tell all the truth but tell it slant," and what Stendahl nailed flat when he wrote that "a novel is a mirror *dawdling* down a road."

I make many of my walks out of squares and rectangles of tinted concrete, which sounds awful but isn't. They are locally made and come in red, black, or tan, each hideous in its own colorful way, but fading is mercifully built into them when their pores fill with soil. Their surfaces become acceptably smooth early on. They are high enough and porous enough to provide a safe, dry footing soon after a shower or a needed dousing, and they are not too heavy to lift and set in place. I arrange them in whatever pattern I choose and as I see fit, rectangles in vertical fours alternating with two horozontals being a repeated design in red, but you might mix colors and shapes if you were after stronger effects. I leave spaces and I don't fill the cracks. In them go *fraises des bois* or thymes woolly and lemon, which get clipped by passage and whose scents get carried indoors. The two-inch height of the blocks makes such injuries superficial and is an inadvertent way of keeping the plants in check. As bordering growth bends over, I move the stones beyond their drip lines and gain another swerve, another meander, another moment to admire a planting in its full, unrestricted habit.

I set the stones on an inch or two of well-rotted manure. Under the paving, roots feed with great vigor throughout this moist, evenly cool, nutritious environment. They also act as firmers. I don't level the ground before putting the stones down, for I like the small elusive shadows that result from uneven paving. I find that a large carpenter's screwdriver is an excellent tool for prying them up. Children like the way the stones go down, and that, I think, is high flattery. But someone older said that my paths were like paths to a privy, and I liked that too.

On heavy-work days I tie back intrusive branches to avoid accidental injury. I use a wheelbarrow with a fat rubber tire. The new sort of much-advertised cart, a rectangular box on two thin bicycle tires, is much too wide for my needs and turns corners awkwardly. It is a good enough device for the open meadow, where it carries large loads steadily and well. But it is too well balanced to be a good wheelbarrow, tipping being what a wheelbarrow should be all about. I have a fine one made by hand by a wise local carpenter. It has oaken handles I rub with linseed oil to counter splitting and is of a venerable design. It is a scalding orange that is somehow entirely appropriate to a green setting. It is a splendid wheelbarrow because it tips on demand and its fat swollen tire moves well. It has an agreeable squeak and it holds a lot or a little. It would be a perfect cart if the closed end could be removed for better spilling. It can be left in the rain, which the other can't. I'm very fond of it. It gets around shrubs and takes bumps with matronly discretion. It brings to mind old Scottish gardeners in Victorian engravings—the types who carried unlit pipes. Muttering surrounded them like midges and they had a fierce urge to cut out and have a pint.

I have had the main path of the inner garden reset. (Into a composition of bordering ramblers and asparagus are wedged white and pink rhododendrons, Russian sage, striped liriope, sea holly, and buffers of astilbe in pink and ivory, all of which are then floated in cushions of specimen grasses, the tone of the garden made immediately apparent.) Trouble was that it is the work path and the wheelbarrow was losing too much on the uneven setts. Ropes were plaited into the tallest of the encroaching grasses, twisting them into heady Dutch hayrick swirls. Out of the way too went main rhododendron branches, tied toward their centers, and beyond some campanula and platycodon that were transplanted, little had to be moved. Nothing at all was broken.

Treated boards were pegged and trenched upright to edge the affair, palest washed sand was spread, to be tamped bevel-flat, and then the bricking was laid in tight patterns. A final thick coating of sand was spread and swept into the cracks, but much was left to be packed by foot traffic for greater firmness. A grand, slightly elevated esplanade resulted, which I'm very pleased with, where tools and baskets and wheelbarrow comfortably may park. All three side routes will remain as narrow and arbitrary as ever, though.

Mine is an American garden with faint tracings of a childhood spent in the woods, where anything moving, anything orange and gold, spoke Indian. I don't hanker after an English rialto, whose high and wide stretches were mandated by an unspeakable climate and fine clothing. The English path was a sort of road, rather, with safe, level, skidproof surfaces from whose borders blooms were handed by gardener or intrepid gentleman (it was a rare lady who snipped her own) stripped of thorn and lower leaf, quite safe for vasing. Those few variants on the form to encourage rambling growth and lavish greens poking between pebbles or brick were rarely emulated. Bushes and plants swayed heavy with wet, and dousing was definitely out. Utility was implicit in all its wide invitations. While masters slept, large carts and barrows preceded a brigade of gardeners, who lifted and set new compositions. They left with the debris when the house woke up. Paths curved in the grandest of sweeps, and the pattern of strolling followed them from the long great hall. High, wide, and dry was the major perimeter path, but this was for horses and traps and seldom for walking.

I think we now have an opportunity for more personal variation. Being wet is not for us so grim or slippery, for we have jeans and sneakers. Because we are freed of various conventions, the garden is no longer a place for serious flirting. We generally walk in our gardens alone, grateful for the privacy. Tugging roses don't call for needle and thread.

Our gardens are much smaller. It is not within our time or means to make a series of outdoor rooms. We are already within our destination, the one large room, rather like the studio apartment we will all eventually live in, where all has got to be carefully distributed and arranged.

In my inner garden, which is almost entirely bounded by the summer house, I lay and relay paths at will, moved by the changing green architecture itself. And something further, undoubtedly a nostalgia for colonial wilderness, makes me want never to be an intruder in my own garden, so none of my paths are concreted and none put too firmly down. I don't want to stop root flow. Since the house is on three sides, its windows on bad days give aspect enough.

Outside this compact area, the roughly clipped meadow is as full of private intrigue, particularly when I decide to mow here and not there, making islands and archipelagoes and moving peninsulas of green. And even in this, possibility is kept open, for there is more than one way to go around. It is another form of the same room, really, the more open part, backed by walls of privet blocking a constantly diminishing view.

Go against it, if you will; we are all headed toward the atrium. What lies beyond our garden walls is unbenign and ugly.

Four years ago I made a short path of grass and lined it at the sides with two- or three-year-old yew transplants (or perhaps they were all four-year-olds). Fed well and watered carefully and mulched often and thickly with a combination of salt hay and peat moss, the little hedge prospered and grew tall and dense. I wasn't at all sure at what height I would stop it, thinking all the while of a dark-walled path, utterly blocking out the seductions of the plantings on either side. It was when a curved stand of blue liriope took off a few weeks ago, and, farther down, Japanese wood anemones (white) next to a stand of joe-pye weed mixed with pink cleomes and white Italian sunflowers, that I realized the hedge had grown far too tall; the flowering cosmopolitan was now graceful and shapely enough to be viewed in the entire.

I cut the hedge down, both sides, lower even than when I planted it, this new height of no more than nine inches sufficient to give a double frame, the bright green grass, the nearly black flatness of the sheared yews almost like a riser on a staircase. The walled feeling I had been after is now on a larger, more distant scale, for behind the flowering plantings on one side are trees and evergreens (deodar), and a stand of yarrow and bayberry on the other. It was like gutting the wall of a room and taking in another room to make of the both one large, aptly proportioned chamber. I am pleased with this. The shearing was difficult and had to be done by hand, using a broken staff of bamboo as a guide. It took the better part of a day. To aid recovery, the yews were soaked for several hours afterward, and now I will place additional mulch. Pruning is a word autumn can never erase.

Seats

THE COURTESIES OF HOSPITALITY are few and fundamental. After thirst is slaked, rest is offered. The first is why gardens have fountains or pools, or at the very least a visible water source with nearby cup. The second is why gardens have seats. When well done, these intrinsics should have high architectural finish, for as much as their use is intended for others, they intimately reflect the eye and the taste of the host. (Gardeners generally get water from a bent hose or an inconvenient faucet, and as for seats, they need them not, for what they do is sink rather than rest, and at such moments a log, lawn, doorstep, wall, or fence, or the very earth, will do, for no bench, it seems, is ever opportunely placed when garden work takes its toll.)

I have gone through innumerable types of seats. Wicker was one for a time, and when love was high a lovely set was left for me before the big pool, with a bright red crayon message: "Santa Claus." June. My birthday. And there they were, three of them, as frail as china, as white and wet as a complicated Edwardian dessert, the stuff of fine terraces, of tea carts with minute watercress sandwiches. And staff.

Wicker takes work, in and out of season. Fine weather and poor, it must be shielded from mold and dirt and enemy damp. Fray points release tiny holding nails which seem to loom with use like silvery fish rising, snapping at flesh and cloth. And as much as white is wicker's only true and perfect color, no white that I coated my set with seemed equal to its allure in old photographs, although through the years I tried medium to high and low glosses and once even an unabashed matte spiced with traces of blue and brown. They blew over in the lightest wind. They were an awfully hard sit without cushions, and these too needed turning and wiping, and so the little set is now a sad little patch in the basement. A memorial to a vanished era of ease and affection.

As if in reaction to it all, there was a brief moment when I tried the pleasant dinkiness of what is called the Adirondack chair, that slat-boarded, plain, no-nonsense native rival of the cruel Bauhaus chair. An infliction and not a comfort, it is most adept at holding wet and loggy leaves, is impossible to rise from gracefully, and gives all sitters a deep, rather stubborn, look, with knees against faces when seen head on. Its only function, it seems to me, is to get into a lot of plein-air American painting, because it has come to be entirely emblematic of summer. Only John Calvin would approve. Adirondack chairs are often seen empty ("The mosquitoes are out!") and look nice so. Their armrests are large enough for drinks but seem always dangerously sloped, and the ground beneath them soon becomes a mess of ashes and butts and matchsticks, because ashtrays slip off too.

As much as the eye of the viewer may be led in gardens, it is through a diffuse set of tuggings or coaxes, a series of mild seductions, each one tethered to another, a series of flourishes embellishing the whole. To point to a single dominant vista in a garden would be a way of erasing all of these little accomplishments, and a bench placed before it would underline such aridity. Seats ought to add to a carefully cultivated and generalized feeling of soft satisfaction of the sort that comes of felicities in chain. They are the strand winning over the pearl. It is one reason that I have kept my garden so full of paths: there is no particular best way to go through it, except that one is always finest for me when the sun is sinking, the one where foliage gets illuminated from the back, the better to see structure. Here there is no bench.

Lettuce Forever

MANY ERRORS AGO, I found that I had purchased nearly two dozen of the world's most famous lettuces. At least the seed catalogues had claimed them to be unrivaled. Throughout a longish winter they had been arriving and soon were in the basement, jammed into an old Huntley and Palmer biscuit box, the lid sealed against the damp with masking tape. They were French and English and German and of course Italian as well as American. Sending money for them had been difficult, involving conversion tables or an extra dollar if I was lazy. There they were, lettuces flat, wrinkled, shiny, and dull; lettuces that splayed out and those that headed in an oval or a round; leaves with tinges of red margins or dark red throughout; early-lifting lettuces and varieties that promised not to bolt or, if they did, to come again from the sides and not be bitter.

When flats of them covered the floor beneath the south window of the winter house, with a system of boards and chairs shielding them from my nosy dogs, and it began to be hard to get to the dining table, and the finish came up from the floor from frequent waterings, I knew that somehow I had to monitor my obsession. But I love salads, and although one can make a salad out of nearly anything, it is lettuce and not arugula, watercress, endive, sorrel, burnet, or spinach that is both its fundament and its keystone, the simple melody from which its many variations spin, and I could not resist a remote German seed firm whose lettuce was billed to be fine for all four seasons, a lettuce *auf wald und feld*. And a Swedish one, vintage King Olaf, the melter of fjords. I will have it wilted for breakfast, I thought, and I dreamed again of a magnificent bell-shaped sculpture of salad greens presented to me in a restaurant in Munich, a high, bright piling of greens club-shaped and fan-shaped, pale green to harsh blue, greens of the wood and of the fields, from which I slowly made my choice and for which I stirred a dressing. Eating it, I forgot Munich itself, a city that made me seriously uncomfortable.

Whatever its purported capacities, a good lettuce is basically a spring crop, and a reprise may be had, if one is cautious as to timing, in late August or so. It should grow fast and never suffer from dryness. It should be adequately spaced and come from a soil free of stone, high in organic matter, and rich in nitrogen.

You can plant lettuce as thick as grass in a row if you will be ruthless with the thinning. Or start plants in individual peat pots indoors and place them doubly heavy in the row and lift the immature specimens when leaves begin to touch. The trouble with the first is that lettuce has a long taproot and is sensitive to jarring; a row of seedlings, thick and pale green, is generally so lovely that one is leery of intruding on it, so, foolishly, one thins from the outside and not the heart. The trouble with the second is that overnight the entire row becomes a solid mass, and one is faced with fifty feet of lettuce, and however much of an herbivore one is, no appetite is equal to it, and one must water beautiful plants.

The hope lies in a bed rather than a row of lettuces, plants set in a lattice pattern, six inches apart, with carrots or beets coming through them for a companionable second crop. In this way, gaps won't seem so wrenching. Scallions or bunching onions through them are nice, too. Best of all I like my lettuces mixed with tulips.

I have not made up my mind yet how vast my lettuce collection will be this year, and I have no favorites, for the taste of lettuce will vary from year to year as much as that of grapes. Or corn. But head lettuces generally have less snap and aroma and cool aftertaste. Leafers are better, the flavor built up by the sun (the mild sun) and the very air. A good lettuce should taste like dew.

Basil

I grow a small-leafed, diminutive, bushy basil that mounds to the ground, is tidy in appearance, and is of a luminous green flushed with lime. It glows as if from some wattage within. Italians call it Greek basil, Greeks are silent about its nationality, and when I can get seeds of it, I find it is called Greek form or Italian form. The Turks are also involved. Whatever its origins, it seems to have more oil—oil of a sweeter kind—than the large flat- or curled-leaf variety. It is easier to manage and doesn't exhibit a distressing habit of losing a stem when burdened by foliage. It has a male and a female form, and both are good for the pot. Like the more robust varieties, it likes warmth and a rich soil and plenty of sun to prosper.

Unfortunately, I lost all one spring when night temperatures dropped below the fifties and the stems went woody and the plants seemed to melt away. I had started a set of twelve indoors around late February in a goodly mix of humus and sphagnum moss laced with sharp, clean sand for stability and handling ease. A dense planting in a tray in the sunniest window—an overly dense planting, for I like to use the prickings in salad. When the true, secondary leaves appeared and consolidated, the plants went into tight little pots and were sheltered for days from strong light to reduce wilt-shock, and then back into the hot, sunny light. A week or two after our average last killing frost (April 23), when the weather seemed inclined to be warmly stable, I set them out in the best loamy tilth and capped them with waxed protectors, the tops of which were snipped off to minimize daily temperature buildup. A few weeks later the caps came off, and then the weather turned back—great for grass and awful for a lot of other things. I was happy to get replacements.

The basil I really don't like and don't grow is the opal kind. It is no good in the border and useless in the kitchen. It is an unpleasantly colored plant, as its purple does nothing but make interruptions or holes in a mixed planting, and one doesn't want this color unless it is far away in the form of a copper beech in someone else's garden. Then it is quite perfect. This basil is frequently used to decorate cold dishes and makes me quite leery, in an atavistic sort of way, I guess, for medical views in ancient times were strongly divided on the use of basil. One group thought not only that it was poisonous but that scorpions grew from its odor.

All basils suffered at the hands of the old Greeks, who thought they represented hate and misfortune and insulted them in order to make them grow. This attitude continued among the Romans, who, large in every one of their borrowed gestures, did not stop at insulting it at sowing time but vilified and railed against it all through its sweet-scented lifetime, the better to make it flourish. Here is a plant, I suppose, on which one might loose one's peeves.

But it was also the herb of fraternity and the gift of sympathy and affection and is still a love token in Italy and was known in Crete as "love washed with tears." Hindus go to paradise with a basil leaf on their chests. Basil is sacred to Krishna.

It is closest to cloves in its scent and is the very odor of high summer. Bumblebees roll from it, leaving tracks of its aroma. Invisible nets of its wild scent seem to hang everywhere in my garden, bringing serious thoughts of spaghetti to the month of August, whose air is exactly that of a kitchen in high gear.

In the autumn, before nights get too cool, I clip back a few bushes severely and prune the roots themselves before potting them up in the same rich seedling mixture. They are kept dark and moist for a few days and then given manure tea for reinvigoration. Basil is so fine when it recovers, a single pot glowing on a winter table.

Celery and Celeriac, Lovage and Smallage

Nothing blows the palate with as broad a register as celery. It is as murky as sage and as alert as parsley, with a lot of the Alps thrown in. Stem, root, and leaf, it is a fine way to soups, vegetables, and salads. But it is the root I care for most, and so I grow celeriac. It being a very long grower, I can harvest some in the fall and pile up mulches to keep the remainder of a short row on friendly terms with hard freeze, available for the kitchen throughout the winter. It is worth considerable tedium to get the goodly knob.

Ten weeks before the last firm frost of spring, I soak the seeds in warm water for two days in a little plastic cup placed in a warm, sunny window. I put a sheet of kitchen toweling on top and invert the container when I am ready to plant. In this way, in careful fashion, the liquid can drain, and the seeds, with their hard shells softened for speedier germination, can be spread over the sheet for picking up with tweezers (or a dry finger) and planted in individual peat pots. And then patience, even moisture, and a sunny window. Celeriac plants have to be strong, stocky fellows before being placed out in rich, deeply dug soil, for they and stalk celery (which is to be started at the same time) must make an early, raring start in the garden or they will suddenly total, or wither slowly, and you will have nothing but the planting holes. Here the secret is a soil high in nitrogen, and you might prepare the bed in autumn by digging in quantities of cured manure or compost with peat moss. Sometimes cultivation for either celery or celeriac is recommended on "mellow ground," which is something I think I understand but have difficulty explaining. Say it is fine tilth, a well-turned, well-nourished, stone-free soil, and there is still a mile to go for the meaning. Both like incompletely finished compost.

Celeriac looks like stalk celery untied but on the thin side, or giant Italian parsley on the fat. It takes room. Because it is the root we want to encourage and it is all too small in comparison with the exuberance of the tops, I suggest that you remove some of the earth around the bulb when it begins to swell and slice away at the mat of fibrous roots. In this way the knob will swell rounder and smoother and there will be less waste when it is lifted and trimmed. But you may not want this bother, and so you may want to skip celeriac and stalk celery and head straight for smallage, which is an easy little plant and whose parts—stem, leaf, and root—are all fine to eat.

A variety of specialty seed houses will supply you with packets of the three of them but, disconcertingly, not every year. A more dependable way of ensuring that you will have the bright taste of celery at all times is to grow lovage, which is an immensely sturdy perennial, quite darkly neat and very lavish in its foliage. One will do, for it is the leaves that go to the pot, unless you want its immense flowering stalk somewhere in the back border, where a rocket of yellow nearly seven feet tall will go aloft in June. I have tried it there and liked it. It is available at local nurseries in spring.

Alliums and Others

Gardening is an act of homage, an accolade to the earth itself. Celebrating it with flowers and flowers only has always seemed a bit niggardly to me, and it is for that reason (in addition to an ample vegetable plot, gooseberries, currants, blueberries, grapes, autumn raspberries, and pear and apple trees) that I intersperse not just herbs in the inner garden but solid bearers of grub as well. Nibbling and sniffling being pleasures too great for only rabbits to indulge in, it has never struck me as queer and odd to have lettuces and roses in the same bed. Chives are in their place now too. They stay alert through the long season because I treat them as the grassy types they are and cut them right down to within an inch of their culm-type basing whenever untidy browning becomes an eyesore. They freshen quickly, and with this procedure, picking them for pot or salad involves less trimming. An occasional bloom after their major spring performance is an additional reward for such sanitation. At the ramblers' base they mask what fallen yellowed leaves I may have neglected to remove, and their other use is to inhibit the proliferation of aphids at the growing tips of canes. Aphids will be there, but not in such revolting quantity.

Another allium of far less rank habit is the garlic chive, which may be happily mixed in the general flowerbed, its long blue foliage a tidy accent and its well-supported umbels of erased gray-whites excellent additions in sun or partial shade. Welsh bunching onions are another splendid member of the immense family, with broad white flowering globes on long sticks in the latter part of spring. They are a permanent supply of scallions but better cooked than raw. I have mine next to the rhododendrons, and the only quarrel I have with them is that their foliage flops, so that I must move them farther back in the border, away from the path; onion juice on shoe leather can take over a house. Each year I plant leeks in the richest soils of the garden, and some are for the pot and some are left over the winter to bloom early next summer, five-foot-high blooms like planets with attendant stars wired to them. Elephant garlic grows in other parts. True hemispheric blooms are all too infrequent in current collections of available garden matter.

Cardoon, a member of the astonishing thistle family, is easily raised from seed indoors in February. Cardoon is the biennial fellow whose stripped stalks you have seen at Italian greengrocers'. You poach it, like celery, then bread and fry or bake. Of symmetrical cushiony habit, its mature leaves are like translucent steel arches. Fresher celadon-silver foliage continually replaces the yellowing. Big in architecture and exuberant, it needs space in which to reveal the way it takes light, holds dew. Although this business of yellowing foliage can be annoying, removing the leaves during the growing season is small fee, easily dispensed.

I have fifty feet of asparagus divvying roses from astilbe, terrace from main path, and after I have done with cutting them, the line fountains most remarkably as it stores up strength for cropping next year. This is a foliage plant of the highest merit. Asparagus may be used in clumps, as specimens, or as a soft, high, smoky green hedge. Because its habits of nutrition are identical to that of roses, a companionable position saves labor.

Now, I would grow rhubarb if I liked to eat rhubarb, for I can see how it might work, the red stems, beads of morning dew caught on the broad leaves. Even so, it is too coarse for the general garden.

Plant matter is plant matter; that is its employment. One considers form first, color second, and use may then come into the conjecture as a most welcome third. Nothing gives me greater satisfaction than a bed of yellow rubrum lilies and ostrich fern under four semidwarf pear trees—all curves and globes and columns. Where I want its special qualities, parsley goes in, the flat, broad-leafed Italian sort, invaluable as a floater. And the grape is lovely enough not to be relegated to beyond the border. And quince. And blueberries, whose autumn habits marry instantly with those of Michaelmas asters. Any of the basil family is beautifully foliaged and delightful in bloom—any except the opal, as I've said, which was bred for its color and is the least ingratiating plant one would want in a garden, and the worst to taste. It grows like an empty violet stain and decorates bowls of edibles like green matter gone bad. Try beets.

Nuts and Berries

The scenario of an edible landscape is as old as Eden. It is strongly in play again, one of the many solid ideas gaining prominence in the canons of gardening's new naturalism. It is as right as mulching, spraying with soap, and composting wisely. It takes cognizance of the tremendous superiority of plant types typical of specific gardening areas, and the gardener need no longer think that tough and hardy, disease-resistant cultivars are necessarily mingy or unattractive. Such plant individuals are immensely suited to present demands for low-maintenance material. Take berries, for example. Gooseberries and currants make fine hedges, and blueberries better ones in the Northeast. Often seen in conjunction with mountain laurel, rhododendron, and azalea in the wild, hybrid varieties are no problem at all if you are successful with the other three.

Blueberries will mount to a fine, thick, six-foot hedge in less time than one might think and are a most welcome substitute for privet. Depending upon choice of type, blueberries have a long bearing season, bare branches in winter are interesting, and the bright blaze of their fall foliage is a stunning addition to any distinguished garden. We will leave them unpruned, except for necessary sanitation and general well-being, and we will never, ever disturb the soil beneath them after an initial drifting of snowdrop, squill, and crocus is all through. Blueberry roots are close to the surface and must be kept damp and mulched. All-white collections of the little bulbs will make a fine showing against its rubbed dusty orange bark, which shoots with tan as it matures. A liberal, thick mulch of peat moss and salt hay is fine for blueberries and spring bulbs, as is bone meal, which is entirely compatible with either. Since blueberries leaf out on the late side, the little bulbs will have ample light to mature their foliage and set buds for a year hence. More than one variety of the bush will be needed, as blueberries do not self-pollinate; three is the bare minimum, I find.

Blueberry bushes are largely insect-free, although birds are a sometime plague. Netting brought to the ground and moored in and spread at the top evenly will often, alas, reap a grim harvest of trapped, broken birds. However, birds seem to get tired of eating the same thing and after initial marauding will take off and attack other berries, or return to insect fare, so I don't net at all. Natural gardening must take into account loss—it is all part of it.

As far as fruits and nuts go, great advances are being made in developing pecans and persimmons, highly underrated, underutilized candidates for the home plot, quite at home in the northern zone. They are strong and lovely trees, both of them, and give shade and agreeable shape with minimum care. Although I wouldn't ever remove a fine old oak for one, I would give hard looks at all my trees and begin to think of replacing those whose performance has always been under par, trees that I have stared at for far too long to have any discrimination left but that I merely accept with affection. These can come out, to be replaced with mulberry or crab apples. In limited space, double planting in one hole is advisable. Double planting will supply dependable cross-pollination when advised, create competitive vigor in both cultivars, and give a venerable, more interesting, less *arriviste* look to the area. Other splendid opportunities lie in the hickory, the walnut, and the filbert, although this last often has barren years, blooming as it does when killer frosts are still possible. There are old apples, as hardy as anything you can plant, with fruit usually smaller than contemporary varieties but infinitely tastier, more dependable, and with good winter keeping qualities. The habit of an apple tree is fine for the small garden. Apples take pruning well and are tolerant of shaping and can be thinned enough so that you might, if you wish, run a grapevine up the trunk, where it will rest and bear on the branches for double bounty. Intelligent pruning is generally all that you need to create fine specimen effects in any of these components of the edible landscape.

I am very fond of the elderly stance of the pear. Moreover, pears are light in leaf, and one may, without worrying too much about heavy canopy, plant a double row down the main garden path for an alley full of intrigue. Clear, shining, pale young leaves are as good to my eye as the blossoms, the drifting of which has sent many an old Japanese quite mad with it all (wine and poetry did the rest). High on the light, raging colors of spring, the Japanese hybridized impossibly huge cherry blossoms and turned the trees into drones, rapacious of root and huge of structure. These have no place in the edible garden. However one may admire them, they are one-shot spectacles and dull and thick after their display. The sour cherry is as good to my way of enjoying spring, with flowers more discreet and a bonus of jam, preserve, and pie fruit later on.

There are many other working trees, working bushes, working vines, fine of foliage, decent of bloom. Each has its employment as a bearer for the table. Winter is a good time to turn to the library, the New York Botanical Garden, the U.S. Department of Agriculture, and your region's arboretum or botanical garden for solid information about edible bushes, trees, and vines. They will supply you with sources, descriptions of recommended varieties, and sound basics of cultivation.

The Autumn Raspberry

At times, my autumn-bearing raspberry begins to throw ripe berries, a few at a time, in the last week of August. By the end of the first week of September, however, the thimble-shaped fruits are getting into production, enough for several small plates or a medium bowl. By week two, they swell in earnest and go on and on, independent of mild attacks of frost. Even killer frosts leave drupes of untouched fruit sheltered beneath the large leaves, seemingly a bit more fragrant for the temperature dip and, under the morning sun, cold and mysteriously intact from their dangerous night.

Raspberries are a northern plant. It is hard to get good raspberries south of Virginia, although in the mountains of Georgia one may. It is not strange, then, that cold weather swells their flavor, and I much prefer late-bearing types, like 'Autumn Gold'. They seem more precious in autumn.

Earlier, they have to compete with the strawberry, and that is a bit unfair.

Raspberry is such a clean fruit. Unlike the dewberry and the blackberry, its near relations, it comes off neatly from its receptacle and is entirely ready for the plate. Those nearly ripe seem ripe enough, and the ripe seem to set unsurpassed standards of fine taste, never staying the palate, rather like that queen of Egypt who Shakespeare thought made one hungrier with each satisfaction.

One never washes raspberries; the dew is enough. All things on the table are made better for them. A single one on a half grapefruit or many over a melon. A raspberry river in heavy cream and that cream poured over a raspberry teacake can silence a whole table. I make salads of young green beans, red onions, and raspberries. Chilled, they are a delirious addition to curries. If ever one's heart thought of stopping, it might be then.

Outside of their tendency to sucker madly, their only problem is in the picking. The lightest bruise (and they bruise easily) leads to mildew. Only a very few, for that reason, can be held in the hand. Use three fingers, not two. Fruit must never be dropped, it must be placed—and placed carefully—in the container and not allowed to roll. A single pecky fruit, or one not entirely fine, can undo a quart. And the bearing canes may sometimes be intertwined and cannot be pulled apart lest all the fruit fall or bruise. The cane may be lifted for easier access, but only so high, and only the softest pressure on the fruit should be used. If a berry doesn't separate easily, it isn't ripe.

Raspberries like full sun, and I would recommend a narrow row rather than a fat patch. One ought to be able to pick a good stand entirely in the round with ease. What to do about this business of suckering—and it can be menacing to the surrounding area—is to think of just how many bushes one wants and either let the row run or each year spade a perimeter and get rid of all roots in the far zone. Even the smallest root will send up a berry-bearing stem, so this is a slow and meticulous chore. I have been throwing mine in hedgerows as an alternate strategy against birds, and sometimes the results are agreeable. Mostly not. Birds, it seems, also cannot get their fill of raspberries.

When birds do descend on the berries, they do so in a most exasperating manner, eating a bit of many rather than all of a few. The damaged fruit is good only for jam. If you do make jam, mix apples in. Not only do they operate as a bit of a stretch, but the mixture is not as all-fired heady as pure raspberry jam, which is head-swimming. A mixture of this sort of raspberry and apple jam with Pommery or de Meaux mustard and Marsala wine, beaten and heated to a boil, is a splendid sauce for duck or cold ham or pork.

A Problem Area

EVERY GARDEN seems to have a problem area, some corner or stretch that never receives a proper solution and remains indifferently achieved or downright unsatisfactory, throwing the rest of the garden's acceptable arrangement into a prominence it may not indeed deserve. Like the dummy at the dinner table, satisfactions get lowered or raised unfairly. One has a tendency simply to pay it far too much attention, almost as if it were an entirely separate problem, which of course it is not. One's overparticularized concern very often throws it out of the frame and into another entirely. The party goes flop and so does the garden.

The front of the winter house and studio is just such a prickled problem. It is rather a spur of the garden proper, being a very narrow strip, a peninsula more or less, jutting out into the surrounding geometries of Foster's farm. It is hidden mostly behind a large berm planted with arctic willows, and when it is visible at all during the summer, it seems to be a broad hedgerow in no way associated with my garden. As such, it is put away from my mind during the growing months, when I am in my other house and studio. But in winter, it becomes the only part of the view that is mine, dead out from the south window, and it is a disgrace. Seeing the area anew as I have each year is of little use in its resolution, for each time it appears to me new and unfamiliar. Not seeing it daily throughout the year, I have not absorbed its particulars. I have, however, been making a major amendment in its general invisibility, first by broadening a path through the copse of black pines, pruning their understory branches so that they spoke up toward the sky and admit into the summer garden the view of its weedy length. The pines, all two thousand of them, are now gone, as are all others in the region, felled by blue spore disease. One side of the spot is now planted with rugosa roses as a hedge. At various times in the past I have planted a few old varieties of apples and have thought of letting it all go back to random field matter, but the resultant tangle of bittersweet, honeysuckle, dog roses, and red cedar made me decide otherwise. I took them all out and had the folly of mind to place another long and oblique berm, intended to echo the first one, using material excavated when I enlarged the winter studio. This got planted with broom, sea buckthorn, spirea, and various random dividends from the inner garden, and for a time the berm was coated in mullein, yarrow, hardiest coreopsis, and *wichurana* roses to unify it all. Which all sounded dilly but hardly pleased my winter eye, and I have just taken the whole mess out.

Where I am now with this gall in my line of vision is to remove the second berm. It has proven to be the least amiable of my mistakes. It was intended not only to function as a windbreak but to interrupt and enlarge upon that area sacred to aestheticians and other purveyors of beauty, the middle distance, a hypothetical construct I find as unnecessary as a jug, say, placed in the far middle of a rug, or a chair out from a grouping and away from a wall. But the berm was also the result of my feeling that the flat expanse in front of the winter window was dull and in need of variation. I see now that it is not. I see now that the true hero of the view is the changing geometry of Foster's fields and that my strip floating out onto them ought to participate in them or anticipate them and show no interruption in the general view, which is one of utility.

So I am preparing an orchard. Not a vineyard, as I had thought, for I must think of the labor hinged on four 125-foot rows of grapes. I like the idea of an orchard more than that of grapes, moreover, for orchards are a nice place to stroll through. Filberts, too, interest me, and I have written to three firms, two in Canada and one in upper New York State, that have been experimenting with filberts, whose blooming pattern is adjusted to frost patterns in our area. (By contrast, the commonly sold Barcelona does not work well out here, having blossoms as premature as peach and thus just as risky.) These, of course, would be one-year-old whips and apt to take a bit of time to bear. I might make a dive for old apple varieties—or equally old pear varieties, which retain shapes quite wonderful when leafless. Meanwhile, I am sinking under catalogues and reference books, and wads of sketches of my miniature fruitery keep piling up. But I have until spring to work it out, and sensibly will shortly turn the whole strip under and plant rye. This winter I will be driving metal stakes through the frost, stretching string, staring at the effect of different spacing, the apples, the pears, the dwarf and semidwarf, and thinking of a berry border going at right angles to the orchard, a row each of currants, gooseberries, and raspberries, with openings through them for long avenues through the trees. Berries leading to fruit, fruit to potatoes; it seems just right. I do hope so.*

*Eventually I went geometrical, echoing the ministrations of the field. A knot garden beneath the south windows; an oval of golden euonymus and eryngium; a 120-foot hooped rose walk narrowing from 8 feet to 6 feet, etc., etc. And at last, at long last, it works!

High Summer

HIGH SUMMER is the time many gardeners look forward to, the time when all of one's plans come full and may be examined by the most acid eye. One's success can never be fudged in high summer. There it is, and the gardener can hardly walk out. He must stay and scrutinize. High summer, however, is when the gardener just might take to his hammock and forget it all. Morose, he lies in all that green.

Or not green. The problem with high summer, and it may be August or it may be mid-July to the end of August, is that tatty foliage often accompanies it. Some of the garden's more prominent and promising specimens get to look a bit worn out by all the growing, and there is much yellow leaf and many lamentable areas in need of pepping up. It is then that a propagating bed may come into play, that bed where things are nursed for next year and robust replacements can be stocked for perking up those areas where things look lost.

In the absence of such a bed, however, other things may be done to blunt the edge of foliate aging, which is quite natural to a whole array of plants. We climb out of our hammocks and take to our shears and give the weary a sound trimming. Columbine and meadow rue are two excellent candidates for this procedure. By the end of July both have flowered and borne seed and, missing cool weather, have rims of wither and pocks of sere scattered in their leaves. I cut both to the ground, and their quick response in the form of fresh, bluer foliage has through the years indicated this to be a sound regimen. Leaves and stalks stay where they fall, adding to the general mulch, and I follow the shock with a half-day of sprinkling.

Groundcovers and all surface rooters sensitive to dryness and heat will also be looking a bit grim. Nothing does woodruff better than a close army trim. Generous and lusty herbs, such as chives, mint, sorrel, lovage, burnet, comfrey, and marjoram, whose fresh, clean new foliage is what the pot and the salad bowl and the eye need, are cut to the ground whenever their leaves darken or show signs of having been aged by strong sun after dew or harsh winds or dryness or simply the beating of one against the other in mild ground airs.

The general tenor of the garden with cutbacks next to mature, untouched specimens is one of greater robustness; one of expectation too, as if pockets of a summery spring had suddenly appeared. High summer is also a good time, if you feel up to it, to go into the hearts of shrubs and prune away April bloomers, but this is mischievous, messy work, full of spiders and moths and errors in tracing the stalks. It is a way of getting a leg up on next spring, but the work may be put off until total leaf fall. As can pruning those few, heavy branches of trees annoyingly distributing shade where you don't want it. Nick the bark to remind yourself of future removal. Or tie a bit of string around where the branch joins the main trunk.

High summer often brings bargain days in the nurseries. Container-grown material may be planted then, and this is, for the northeast coast, a far better time than late autumn, which I don't recommend at all. Prepare the hole beforehand, soak it well, let it sit, and then decant the newcomer into it and water, water well, again. In full leaf, small shrubs and trees will do splendidly, throwing out stabilizing roots, and perhaps flushes of growth will develop early enough to harden and ride the winter out. I would shade the transplant for a few days. Pitch long cuttings of privet or goldenrod stalks in a circle at forty-five degrees all around and tie them at the top, rather like a wigwam.

Balled and burlapped specimens are riskier. These have been standing in the nursery since spring, and one will find that the burlap at the base has rotted and that the earth ball has been considerably disturbed, whether new burlap has been wrapped around it or not. I would take extra pains with these, staking even small acquisitions, giving them more days of shade and almost continual fine, misting spray.

Or you can treat high summer as pure reward, pick blueberries and raspberries, admire what you wish, and ignore the failures. It is up to you whether your feet are up or down. There are all those books you haven't had time to read. More than a few gardeners let their gardens go. I find this hard to do. I like my garden to go on and on. I am into the hearts of almost everything, pruning away.

June gardens are so bright and shining and clear that they seem incapable of aging. Their physicality is everywhere beguiling, and as much as they are demanding gardens, as much as the gardener must be swift with all his work, there is so much joy in it, the stripling growth is so responsive to the smallest of ministrations, that his fatigue seems to get submerged by elation and is at most a fugitive thing. It is satisfying to bend and tie the first long cane of a rose, plot and space a little park of sticky cleome, try new plantings in new beds, see last year's seed-grown clematis take off and throw bloom after bloom. But the slowing is equally rapid.

By mid-July and all through August a gardener's chores are without innovation and become large in repetition, the same thing done at the same spot, over and over. Maturity is in the green frame of the garden and work is entirely custodial in nature, rather like housekeeping, a matter of spit and polish, and the higher your standards, the more minute the work. If there are enough pale or white flowers, the full evening hours may become the only truly pleasing ones. It is cooler then. Deadheading, pinching, pulling crabgrass from paths and lawn, watering, watering, watering, sweeping terraces, are chores done in stillness and heat. One feels like a moldy figurine in a terrarium. One thinks of letting it all go and waiting for September.

But so many unexpected felicities remain as one passes from bush to bush, composition to composition, through vignettes of ingratiation one planned so carefully during the long winter months. It is certainly a time for the chaise, but the thing seems to stay permanently soaked from the sprinkler. Three perfect, perfectly ripe tomatoes come in on a morning, but then fifteen by the end of the week, twenty the next, and then the birds mercifully begin taking pokes at them and one stops trying to fob them off on one's friends (potato bugs will take care of the rest later). One waits for the sound of thunder and sudden ill winds and begins to track Caribbean storms as they coalesce and dart toward the eastern seaboard. Birches seem more singed than in other years, and their leaves and willow leaves are down everywhere. And then the single ginkgo one moved last autumn suddenly breaks from its deadwood in the last week in July to resurrect one's feelings. One remembers that this is the way these trees behave when they are transplanted with any root injury at all. An enormous thistle shows purple and is flecked with pairs of finches streaming through the stems searching for nesting down. When they find none as yet, they loop to Queen Anne's lace, as if anything white might do.

One thinks of dense, satisfying, deep and cool salads, but lettuce has once again bolted, and sprouts from later plantings are still too small. Arugula is doing well, but heat has deepened the flavor and made it terribly sharp. One makes alarming mixtures of chard, fennel tops, parsley, central young leaves of endive, feathers of burnet, and great chunks of white, entirely sweet onions. Young garlic is sliced in lengths from root to stem through the blades like scallions. And some bell peppers, no matter how small.

Days are dry, dusty, but mornings soak in fog and dew. Mornings have odors, noons do not. The *Magnolia grandiflora* has two more buds left, and three *liliiflora* magnolias are out for the second time, but their flowers blister and scald in the sun. By eight the sky is pale metal and a curious wobbling and rippling seems invested in the horizon—a roll of more heat. More dust settles on the leaves of bergamot, but this darkening makes the blooms seem brighter. Catbirds have taken the last of the currants from the new hedge near the new terrace, and one thinks of changing the pattern of the tiles on the old, which now is hardly ever used. Or of covering the stones in a sheet of water a few inches deep, as if a clear spring had welled there. The umbels of elephant garlic are higher by a foot and, beaten down by wind or not, quiver with bees.

Mid-July through August the garden seems to be a thick, stodgy parade, with all of its outlines dulled and clouded. It seems to lumber along, muffled in too much rich living, and its greens begin to mature and shade like drifts of snow in January twilight. I don't know quite why, but optimum foliage has always rather bored me, perhaps because ends for me have never been as important as the means one employs to achieve them. It is like the long, fat summer book whose passages one hoped would go on forever but whose theme gets to seem a drowned or buried thing. A simplicity seems lost or covered. In the streets the world is similarly costumed. Neither birds nor cars nor machines nor people are still. A pageantry, if you will, sometimes lovely, sometimes not. It will be over soon. Pods of seeds are forming. I have seen sweaters.

Slug Control

STARING AT THE VEGETABLE GARDEN didn't help. But neither did working in it. It had been a bad year, the worst I could recall. Two factors mitigated against its usual lush mid-August appearance, freakish weather and the lack of mulches. The first one might call dependably chaotic, while the second was a calculated form of slug control; I was tired of providing them with a safe haven. A long, too cool spring, followed by too many nights when the thermometer touched fifty and then down below it. A historic June drencher. Arid heat. Then muggish times and no rain.

Lettuce bolted. Seeds even of chard were swept away, and second and third plantings gave spotty germination But I did have a few successes. Nice long French yellow beans. A handsome harvest of elephant garlic and red-skinned garlic, which is sometimes called 'The German'. Peas thrived, getting out pods and filling them before strong heat. Beets looked all right, but crack marks showed where the globes were above soil, fissured by the sun.

Only some leeks seemed husky enough to go into their ramparts and swell enough for winter digging, and all the celery was catastrophically slow, stuck in its growth pattern.

Fennel, though, feathered well, and little-leaf basil recovered from the early chill, but not the large-leafed basil and not the lettuce-leafed sort. Pointy *fraises des bois* went through it all with undiminished generosity (so small a plant for all that giving!) and the picking was fine, for the birds were off blueberrying and taking the late raspberries just as they ripened.

Like children in the rain who are determined not to come in but stand at the door staring, in a grouch, the vegetable garden had a crushed, minor, stubborn look. The tropicals, peppers and tomatoes and eggplants, had hardened, woody stems, and nutrition was not getting through them properly. Cut-and-come-again lettuce did so and got as bitter as hen food and was pitched.

The currants and gooseberries I planted at the corners did so well in their first year that I seriously thought about letting them have the whole vegetable garden, I was so disgusted with it. But gardeners are perseverers, stout when times are thin, and by February I was once again crowding myself out of the winter house with trays on loading platforms and tomatoes, peppers, eggplant, lettuce, celery, and leeks growing in them.

I went back to mulching the next year; it is the finest stabilizer of climate there is. Once again I provide the slugs with happy breeding grounds; once again I go out by flashlight and pick off the slimy miserables and drop them in jars of salted water. Once again I am scrubbing and scrubbing, working at removing their viscous slime from my hands. But the vegetable garden has returned to its flourishing condition. Salads are simple and uncomplicated matters, leaves taken from the outer bouquet of the plants, a few eaten while picking, the flavor of cold wet dew on a morning lettuce leaf better than coffee or grapefruit juice and toast and jam.

PLANT PORTRAITS V

Gilbert Wild's Daylilies

ONE SPRING I planted a large bed of daylilies in meadow soil cleared of dog roses, honeysuckle, and the oriental bittersweet vine that makes for green hell out here. Although we used bulldozer and muscle, stragglers still send up lusty shoots. Daylilies were what I wanted all right, but of one or a few colors. The problem was that on reading Gilbert Wild's exhaustive catalogue, I couldn't decide on which. The photographs were clear, but off, I suspected, on all hues, and his descriptions entirely too promising for each and every possibility. I broke a fundamental rule and ordered a collection of a hundred varieties, at definitely a bargain price. They arrived on time, were beautifully packed in a crate lined with straw between the layers, and were all individually labeled with nice wooden tags.

My thinking was to keep careful records, choose an amenable four out of the gaudy spectrum, and destroy the rest. Runny rainbows belong in the sky and interrupt sweeping effects. Shrill is not what one wants in a garden. I had hopes for 'Serene Scene' and 'Silent World' but many misgivings about 'Wild Vista', 'Chatter of Color', 'Little Tyke', 'Ringlets', 'So Behave', 'Techni Star', and (oh my) 'Tinkerbell's Petticoat'.

But they have all worked out, each and every one as it comes into bloom, for I think that what I ordered was a collection of Mr. Wild's rejects. I do not mean that they were wizened little performers or substandard plants, but that they were flowers whose colors were pale shadows of leading contenders for daylily stardom. They are varieties that never quite made it. Pale washouts that they are, they have become an appropriate solution for a bed seen through the trunks of magnolias and ginkgoes against a hedgerow, where distance rolls in from the fields and a patch of ocean spume is sometimes momentarily suspended. They are all fine and modestly robust, with foliage that gives in the air, light and feckless and an afterthought of those vagrant random fields where daylilies look best.

As yet the bed is not viewable or photographable, being in its early, skimpy stages. The daylilies are planted a good two feet apart, but a season or two will do for filling in. The ever-present hay mulch is doing a good job in dry times, and bittersweet rising from the smallest chips of orange stems sends up fewer shoots.

The daylily is like a good old wooden house chair of firm construction and sturdy, pleasing appearance. One could easily make an entire garden of them, although that would be my idea of gathering hell, for recent innovations bloom early to late, right through hard frost. Some have scents of a soft crispness. Daylilies and hollyhocks and rugosa roses, with spring bulbs aplenty, and one might be home free, with Grandmother's house in the distance.

With thanks to Gilbert H. Wild & Son, whose deductible catalogue is $3. Write for it at P.O. Box 338, Sarcoxie, MO 64862, or call 417-548-3514. They have fine irises and peonies too.

Monkshood Blues

For many years I grew monkshood and for a few I didn't, for it was a pack of woe, and I believe that one shouldn't grow what doesn't do well in one's garden. Monkshood was certainly not doing well in mine. At best, I found it untidy in a stiff way. At its worst, it had the grim habit of seeming to flourish and then, unaccountably, sickening to the point where it stood like sin or bad weather. It got blight and it got mildew and it finally got me down and I pitched several clumps into the rhododendrons, where it got layered under a few mulchings. Exile, not banishment. I forgot about it. Oh, not entirely, for I saw its leaves from time to time through the wholesome foliage of the rhodos, which masked, I knew, the loathsome condition of the rest of the plant. And now the clumps are blooming again. Having taken the requisite several years to recover from dislodgement, they seem to have straightened up and decided to do fabulously well. At least, according to their visible parts. Now I have five-footers bearing blue helmets above the bushes as if rising for oxygen while treading water in a rhododendron-colored sea. It is a rather perfect composition. The long, ungainly growing is invisible, and the blooms stay fresher in the shade.

The choice of monkshood in America is limited usually to one, but it is a welcome blue. European gardens sport yellows and whites and bicolors and monkshood with bulges and attenuated peaks in their caps. There is even one with a tendency to twine, and one seven-foot horror. Monkshood is a large genus of more than one hundred species. European seed companies can supply you with the missing varieties, and they are not difficult to germinate. Their prime caveat, once bedded, is "never move." The second is that although the plants are perennial, the individual stalks are not and die utterly, to be replaced by sister shoots, which may then take a year or so to bloom.

My rhododendron bed is home to a collection of similar difficult numbers. I have *Clematis recta* there grown from seed. Not truly an upright for long, it is basking quite nicely on the lower branches of the shrubs, where it blooms gorgeously and then displays a continuous flow of bluish foliage, fine on this sort of dark perch. A few old roses, which have a tendency to spindle, also rest on the shrubs and are part of that large group of performers that need foliage masks and should not be seen entire.

If you should grow monkshood, be advised that it is said to have been invented by Hecate and is, in truth, one of the deadliest poisons there is. Medea is supposed to have erased Theseus with it. Witches mixed it with belladonna as a flying ointment. Indians of the subcontinent poisoned wells with it and thus stayed the advance of invaders. It is no good to believe that it is a counterpoison, despite some evidence for that—it is stronger than prussic acid and works very quickly indeed. In the last century, an English hostess was said to have mixed it in with the horseradish and polished off a table of disagreeable guests. She got off, although I find it hard to believe that she could have confused the roots before grating them, and anyone who grows it near edibles is up to little good. It was familiar to the old Anglo-Saxons, who called it *thung*, as they did all deadly plants. Its other name is wolfsbane. It did keep away wolves, with arrows tipped in its juices.

As I write this, I am inclined to pull my clumps up again and deliver them into permanent exile. But I like their October blues, and what I don't have anymore is horseradish.

Tansy

A stand of tansy near the pool has begun to butter, or is it the color of a simple egg, sunnyside? No matter. Tansy is one of those slow but jolting yellows we tend to forget, with foliage so dark it seems evergreen in the border, entirely reliable and frazzle-proof. Its advent preludes goldenrod. It comes out with the wild and cultivated mulleins and replaces golden yarrow, not yet in its last fade. Tansy is one of the few flat-tops whose flowers slide from peak bloom into entirely acceptable, diminished colors. (So does yarrow.) It is a platter flower, slicing dark against other stems when viewed from the side and beaming better than reflectors when seen from above—which is a bit of a problem for most of us when the tansy gets to full stature, but a breeze will toss it toward the eye, like a golden Frisbee, slanting. A tough performer and a splendid one, with deeply scissored leaves, archipelagoes of husky green, and a manageable propensity to wander underground.

Tansy is best grown in large colonies, never as single units, for it intersperses and flops, and its habit and shade can be damaging to other plants. A full slice straight down with the spade all around the colony will expose the wandering explorer stems, which come out easily enough.

I do so in the spring or in the fall or when I have time for it during its growing season, and this bit of extra grooming seems a minimal fee for all its dividends. Things look well against it when it is leafing up, and when it blooms it doesn't overwhelm more reticent flowers. It means to be where you want it to be, however, and permanently, and then it will be there forever. I put it against a field of goldenrod, where it is slowly taking over. The mystery is why, for all its commonness in older gardens, it is rarely seen now.

Although its Latin name, *Tanacetum*, is often listed as being doubtful, tansy remains what it always has been—the herb of immortality, its older root from the Greek *athanatos*. It was so good for keeping flies away that it was used to preserve the dead. And meat in general. It lasts so long in flower and it takes hold of stubborn soil so well that it does seem bent on perpetuity. It was given to Ganymede to make him immortal. Its other name is buttons.

It has a pleasantly bitter smell, but that may just be what immortality is all about—nice, but hard to take. I have heard that it will make you invisible for one day of the year. Invisible *and* immortal. That is a ghost, is it not? No matter. A bunch hung upside down in a tool shed will keep the flies away, exactly as tansy did duty as a strewing herb for the long English hall, which was always a mess of dogs and quarrels and wars and manure and grease from dropped bones and similar examples of rambunctious Anglo-Saxon manners before the island got so very tame and dull. (This occurred when class was invented as a less murderous indoor blood sport.)

Tansy is a good gold substitute for goldenrod if you are allergic to goldenrod and don't grow it, even if you know goldenrod is not the offender and ragweed is and choose to remain sneezing. Goldenrod leaves do often carry ragweed pollen, but not tansy, whose leaves are so deeply inverted, pollen has no way to stay. Accidents may, of course, occur. As my dear friend Mrs. Jock French observed, "There is a serpent in every Eden."

Should you find tansy in someone's garden, ask for a root. It is so tough it may be dug at any time. Cut the stem entirely down to save energy for the transition and place it in any soil except too wet, giving it full sun if you can and half if you cannot. And room. And backing.

An old Easter custom was to give a tansy cake to the winner of a handball game played between men of the congregation and archbishops and bishops. In full vestments, I wonder? Quite a sight, vestments flying and then the golden tansy cake.

CLEOME

Cleome went out of fashion about fifty or so years ago and only now seems to be making a full and welcome return. Its odor probably did it in then and may cause a similar dismissal now. Although it is of an odd and intriguing growth pattern and related to the caper, its other name is stinking clover, which is a bit of a puzzlement, for clover is not what it is about but rather fat, angry skunks spraying into vats of naphthalene.

Crown imperial (*Fritillaria*) comes closest to its scent in the spring but is rather mild in comparison and a bit feral and thrilling. Cleome is the very pit of noxiousness and is best planted at a distance from the path. I would turn it loose in a field and let it seed each year and revert to the all-purpose sort of magenta (but not quite magenta) or blue (somewhat closer) or pink (if it were mixed in the preceding two hues) that most second-generation annuals give in to. Indeed, one sometimes comes across fields in the Northeast where it has done precisely that.

I have the reverters, but each year I also grow 'Helen Campbell' because it is an immensely desirable white and shows off very well in the muddled field. There are, however, certain pink forms that open pink and by noon fade to a fairly acceptable white. Late cool spells will bring on the sulks and then they will look quite awful, but returning warm weather reinvigorates them. They stop in the same halt during very dry spells and recover as quickly when moisture is abundant. The thing about them is that the flowers and the leaves are cut so sharply. The foliage has the habit of aging an old bled-out sort of green of the kind that looks awful on outdoor furniture but grand in a leaf. The plant bushes and is constantly flowering. If you are of a lazy turn, do not start cleome indoors; you can seed it where it is to grow, but then you will have flowers later, and one does want them first thing in August, despite spines (mostly on the base) and a disagreeable gumminess of foliage and stem. And the odor.

Mallows

As large as a fully opened *Magnolia grandiflora*, pink mallows seem made for children. I have a photograph somewhere of number-two godson, Kimmy Esteve, in a red nightdress, squealing with delight at a mallow looming over his head, tilted down. I recall that he toppled backward without harm and sat there for a long time having a very intimate, jolly talk with it, full of clucks and gurgles and cheeps. It was the sort of communion the youngest of the young have with kittens, puppies, and frogs. When he was sent for his nap, he turned at the door and waved at the flower. Was it that the leaves are felted top and bottom? For he kept patting them. Did the large flower glow like some face bending over his crib? All of the faces of childhood do get blurred, and they might as well be flowers, I suppose.

All parts of the mallow are edible in one way or another, and it is so great a healer that Pliny wrote, "Whosoever shall take a spoonful of the Mallows shall that day be free from all diseases that may come to him." Its many other names give some indication of this universality: mauls, mallards, Schloss tea, cheese, and mortification root. "Cheese" for some reason refers to the seeds, which were boiled and eaten. The flowers were strewn before the door but not in the hall. Or they were picked for wreaths and garlands on a clear fine day, after night dew had dried. Mallows decorated the graves of friends. Egyptians and old Chinese ate them, and Syrians too, but they were a famine food mostly. The Bible (Job 30:4) lists mallow as food, although the plant described just might have been purslane or orach. Its roots were boiled and then fried with onions, and the huge amount of mucilage in them made an ideal component of poultices and cough syrups. I am sorry that there is no mallow in a marshmallow, although at times I say there is, for I think that once it might have substituted for gum in that mixture of flour, egg albumen, and sugar.

The best location for this fine summer bloomer is as one finds it, at the margins of marshes and ponds and other still waters, where it is mixed with cattails and horsetails and yellow and blue flag and often pink or white roses. Blue globe thistle makes a good partner, and I have a mallow next to a holly. As much as it prefers standing wet, any decently moist spot in the garden in fullish sun will do if ample peat moss and mulch are provided. One might place it next to a hose outlet if there is a drip, or near an unguttered roofline of the house. If the house is entirely guttered, then perhaps the drain spot will do. One may sow mallow from seed in the spring, but it takes from cuttings quite well and from root offsets in the autumn too.

CLETHRA

I must go after a large clump of sweet pepperbush (*Clethra alnifolia*), that hallmark scent-giver of Northeast woods, in July and August. I planted it under the drip line of the unguttered summer studio before I made the ponds, it being a moisture lover. Now it is time to spread it to the three ponds I have. Sweet pepperbush grew at the shore of my family's lake house, and after pickerel and sunfish had spawned beneath it, its reflected flower spikes would open us all to the heart of summer with a pale sweetness that haunted the whole garden and half the lake. Clethra has a vigor and a constraint bred from adapting to the brunt of bad weather. Its dark green, brilliant leaves emerge late, when the temperature settles, off tough branches able to take ice storms without snapping. In autumn, its foliage, late to drop, goes all the way through yellow before taking and holding on to gold. Its blooms are tapered into discrete lilaclike trusses, cream to bone, unwreckable in thunderstorms, opening not all at once but in slow stipulations, the odor evasive yet quite enough to stop me in my tracks. Lost once in the woods near our old house, I knew I was near water when I smelled clethra, and made my way by it toward a swamp and from the swamp, clethra after clethra, down a small sluggish feeder stream to the edge of the lake. In the dark. My passage was without fear, for the night was calm and the odor guided me as firmly as if it had been a rope stretched from home.

The native variety should be planted more. The hybrid trinket on the market now is a thoughtless pink, and pink is not what clethra is about at all. If anything should be done to the clethra, it might be to produce a type that suckered less and could thrive in a dry situation. But all in all, clethra is fine the way it is. Bugs are not its bane, nor does it ever need pruning. At times one might thin it out, I suppose, if such be one's pleasure, but immediately after it flowers, for it blooms on wood a year old.

I think at one pond it will merge well with a volunteer bayberry, and at another I will set it among cattails. At one I will set it entirely alone. Eventually it will bend over the water and hold it dark there, and goldfish and frogs will go into the shadows and be cool.

THE GARDEN TOUR

THERE IS A MOMENT when products of the imagination come under scrutiny, and like books or paintings, gardens too. These get opened and toured, and as any lawyer or juror could tell us, observation is a funny thing, so open to misunderstanding or assumed interpretation that what is there might just as well not be there. Fair and wide open for all to see, a garden, like a painting, becomes the property of the viewer, as much as the food on his plate—and as incorporated into the prejudices of his body and mind. What he sees is tempered by what he comes with or arrives expecting to see. In this way, I suppose, he makes his own explanation in front of the finished product to protect himself from its exclusivity and make it unfold. The finished thing seldom shows how it began or what went into its polish. The true lover of painting, poetry, and gardening—disciplines that the old Chinese practiced as if they were one—is generally much more interested in how the results got that way. He is the one who looks for notes on the manuscript, preliminary sketches of the painting, keeps his eye on where the trowel has just been.

The thing about opening one's garden is that one must bear this in mind and do the explaining first. I always think that it is a good idea to start a garden tour with a description of the fundamentals of the garden's manufacture. "In 1967," I say, "I started the garden, and there was nothing at all here before that except wild meadow grass, or a mixture of grasses mowed down and made into a meadow. I began the first part of the garden in the center of where I had made the house fold, creating a cove against the wind. Everything that you see has been planted since then. I do the work myself. The only fertilizer I use is five annual truckloads of horse manure and about thirty bales of salt hay, and no sprays whatever constitute the regimen. If a plant seems to object to this and doesn't thrive, it is moved to another location and tried another season. If it doesn't do well then, that plant is pitched and I do not grow it. I do persist in trying sometimes to grow things that clearly don't belong here, but that is my foolishness. And now let's have a look."

Sometimes, though, I might as well not say it, for it simply doesn't sink in. I suppose I should take incredulity as a compliment. My garden is quite healthy, and a lot is packed into its small area. Many visitors think I have a vast staff concealed in one of the sheds together with a large repertory of fertilizers, sprays, and systemics, like a crucial element in a recipe that a cook will sometimes forget to mention. But this is how I garden. Over the years of gardening in this way, finding out what varieties will do for me and not do for me and maintaining soil fertility and soil condition through natural means, eschewing fungicides, pesticides, herbicides, and their ilk, a nice little commonsense cosmos of health has resulted. Birds, toads, frogs, and snakes do the work they are supposed to do, and my fingers do the rest. When slugs get out of hand under mulches in the vegetable garden, new mulches don't go down, and old ones are lifted.

Disasters do occur. That is natural. I have a large weeping willow that is suddenly struck by a virus. It is going. Perhaps on the main trunk I will plant a wisteria, perhaps not. Sanitation will demand the removal of all of it. And then I will see what the empty space looks like, and perhaps the tree will not need replacement. Perhaps the privet around it is really all I will need, when it responds to increased sunlight and freer root run. Perhaps a falling form was all right in that spot when the privet was young, and perhaps now that space could better use a single darkish spire, like a nice, fat, gloomy American red cedar. But what I will not do is run after the books and find a specific, a nasty medicine that will kill the virus, for anything added to a natural garden in the way of a new and complicated chemical cannot avoid roughing up the equilibrium I have been at pains to create.

I use a limited palette in my studio and get all the colors I need from it. Anytime I have enlarged it or changed solvents, the results have been peculiar. The procedures of the garden are really quite similar and just as simple. Manure, salt hay, no sprays, perhaps a teaspoon of lime for the clematis, and oh yes, bone meal, I did forget that, when planting bulbs. If I had extra hands, I would tell them the same.

❧

August is definitely not the month for a garden tour, but August 12 was the date, and I did very much hope for rotten weather. A windy, dark afternoon, with washes of cold Atlantic air and enough rain to keep visitors looking out the windows (for the house was on tour too), might have suited the rather unappealing state any garden drifts into in August. Or a ground fog might have blurred all the things I hadn't done yet, giving softness to foliage already hardened and fresh grace to all of those greens showing signs of brown and red livery.

An August garden is lush but withery in too many spots to give pleasure, and while not entirely convalescent, is nonetheless set out with stakes for the weak and ties for the laggard as if it were, and seems far too close to the sickbay to stand much pleasurable inspection. August is marking time before the next push. Greens will once again be as pale as in May, and the growing, however brief, as roaring to the spirit as in the best month of spring. August begins the time when late raspberries swell, tomatoes pink, and all of those roses that remount come out once again, in less profusion but deepened hue, more finely and intelligently produced, to my way of thinking, than the bushel-barrel effect of late June. But August lasts far too long. It is as long and as dull as January. The same errors of attention seem to come to the fore (prune!), and I walked around tidying and clipping, rather despising the garden and wishing to put little signs of apology all over, or perhaps photographs of each section at peak performance.

The nice groundsmen of Guild Hall came to hammer in red stakes, and on them arrows on posterboard were thumbtacked. A sign at the last door of the house read, I think, PROCEED SLOWLY AND MIND THE UNEVEN PATHS. There were two stakes among the many with two arrows pointing in opposite directions, for at those points one could choose between two ways. Other ways were blocked by wheelbarrows or pots. The two far beds I had still not had time to attend to, and I hoped the view beyond their borders would make eyes less discerning. And then a nice volunteer came with a card table and chair and set them up in the studio. And then another hostess arrived and more red stakes went in, down at Main Street, and I could leave, with hundreds of feet of hoses coiled and stacked, every outdoor pot with bunches of the blooms of leeks, picked just at the point when they were beginning to fall and could be culled for display. And then I went to do errands I had put off since June.

Rather like being on exhibition, giving over one's house and garden for a house and garden tour is an awfully final transaction. What one has been doing in utter privacy loses all of one's proprietorship, and the making of the place remains invisible, only a stage of it seen. As if one were signing a deed of transfer in a lawyer's office, one goes away from it full of misgiving, more than a little unsure, very much wanting the thing back. The fact that I would indeed get my place back didn't spark me at all, for during a four-hour tour, what I had done in the house and in the garden and what was on the walls of the house and the walls of the studio were going to be judged. Any form of judgment, even the mildest sort, is really a very terrible thing.

The morning had started out shifty and wet but cleared by eleven, and by twelve forty-five, when I left, the sky was developing blues, puffed with clouds getting steadily drained of gray. White and clear they began rising on the horizon, and whiter still they began sailing past. I found myself needing high reward—or was it assuagement of contradictory feelings?—and bought a very expensive electric hedge cutter, my Calvinist side rebelling. Weren't hand shears enough for the long hedge of childhood, and what is the hedge I now clip but a replica of it? Hand shears ought to stand me now in good stead, the continuity of humble, repetitious labor being always the honored prerequisite for correcting errors of the soul, good for a muddy spirit, bracing for a wandering mind. Labor-saving devices run counter to all that.

I drove through several towns, dispatching errands at stores, and came back at fifteen to five to drop off two pints of ice cream in the freezer. For blueberry pie. I was giving a dinner for eight that night. I waded in through visitors and went back outside to my other house to get the dogs. Groups were all over, talking and pointing, the day clear on them, and it was nice to see. I have never seen so many people smiling, gently enjoying themselves. They were taking their time, seemed to be kind about all my errors, and were warmly focusing on the few solid achievements. An old-fashioned approach, I thought, rather like the way people in museums used to give pale, reticent paintings a chance to grow. Whether it was the day or the garden that was doing the wooing, I wasn't sure, but they were enjoying themselves, and I found pleasure in that and in answering the questions of those who took my stance for ownership, the chief one being "Who takes care of all of this?" I felt a little like answering, "Not I."

Fifteen hundred people came through the house and the garden, and when they left there was not a flower picked, a shrub broken. The very grass seemed as smooth as the post–Labor Day beach drained of summer, almost more beautiful than before, as if enhanced by all the use. I have the card table and chair, still not picked up. They seem warm and friendly. I have been thanked over and over again for giving my place to the tour, but it is I who have had the larger gift. I have seen what it is all about, this little life of ours. Much work. A moment for a visit. And then, away.

Late Summer Skies

Late summer skies are frequently of that unphotographable blue that memories are made of, harvest blue with white stringer clouds that migrating birds breach with punctuation, and the days are at last truly domed and perfect for walking—but they are shortening. We now enter into an ever-narrowing tunnel toward December, when the light will go down in mallets under hard, unhumid skies. I have been working right up to and through the rapid dusk, and I find I must leave tasks unfinished until the next day, and some I realize I must defer even longer, so many and urgent are the demands of late summer.

But the colors of this kind of dusk are so intriguing that one evening I made a path of ground-hugging variegated euonymous, a little ripple of silver between blue plumbago (more October than September blue) and perennial salvia, whose blues go a bit into wet-litmus-paper violets. My eyes in the dusk liked the idea, and I was delighted to find it just as intriguing the next day, and to find that I didn't have to relift the plants, for I was looking at twenty-four bales of salt hay waiting to be spread and four double truckloads of manure. And with the crocus bulbs, ever-beguiling *Iris danfordiae,* an iris that explodes earlier than crocus, has arrived in the mail. All have to be carefully planted, in those spots I have learned that the sun first warms next end of winter (and even in midwinter, if we have a decent January thaw). Crocuses look fine backed by yews, but the irises will be set without backing, being less translucent, and pebbles will be their base. Mulches of salt hay are too smothery for their impertinent posture. I will plant them next to the studio door, where no cultivation goes on, and they will multiply there, as have others I put in some years ago. Of their many rewards, the best is the discretion of their foliage, so modest that its ripening is a nearly invisible process. Bulb bloom is a welcome gift, but the later withering of the foliage as it matures is so much torn wrapping. I plant most next to clumps of perennials and bushes, where their duties of ripening get quickly obscured. Daffodil straps I have always cut down, though, when half yellow, with no discernible difference in future flower crops.

And then I had an enormous welter of slashed prunings lathered about the base of everything, and this is always best left for a few days until it loses its pounds of water and is easier to lift or drag away. I build up the hedgerow with it in hopes of making decent hiding for nesting wildlife. But the straightest of the culls I strip of laterals, for they make fine poles for beans and peas.

Although most of this is done with a hand anvil pruner, all other needed tools are with me in the wheelbarrow (a trug is too small), and they are in twos. There is the tool in the hand or the one in range of the eye, and then there is the similar one always drowned in the falling green, and one can't take the time to poke for it. Different cutters for different tasks. I am very fond of a curved Japanese saw in its wooden sheath. It is efficient and near to being lethal and I need only one, for it has a fine leather snap that exactly moors it to my belt. I also use a long-handled parrot-beaked lopper for higher, harder work and an ordinary saw, a hatchet, grass shears, and hedge cutters.

Of course I could wait for cooler weather, but cooler weather will mean other chores. The schedule of the garden is quite rigid, and any part of it unobserved leaves all the rest fumbled and in improper kilter.

If I am being unkind to August, it is chiefly because it is an overly generous month with often chancy gifts. It bulks large in its givingness, like a filled and foamy pocket with an ever-enlarging rip. I had a spell of triumph when frost-inhibited eggplants began to bear beautifully and then too much. Violent weather followed the still with rain in clumps so that minidroughts called for continual watering. And then an eerie, early chill came in, with mist all over the fields. August was, as usual, every pot going.

The Fall of Summer

IF AUGUST is a brat and a half, it is doubly obnoxious when it brings its freaky, high-strung behavior well into September. All by itself, it is a vile little season divorced from the generally satisfying nature of summer, an unnerving time as dismal as its calendar counterpart, January. If it wants to be hot, hot it stays. Or cold. Or rainy. Woven through all of its tiresome behavior run wild temperatures and sudden storms with sheering winds. Chairs topple. Branches and stems whirl and break. Most foliage can't take it, and the terraces and the walks are piled with torn and mildewed remnants. It is a time of bugs tunneling into fallen fruit, pulled onions that take too long drying and begin to root again, and crabgrass as lusty as bamboo. Except for the mallow and the cleome, the late summer garden is an almost empty interval between the time that thistles blow and when cooler nights and brighter weather freshen buds on the roses and call forth clean new foliage from all the things I cut down when they were sere and bedraggled.

I am never sorry to see August go. I often spend the major part of its bell-jar humidity far from the hammock, in the shrubbery, bruised and sweating, pruning Amazonian growth. August is when I excerpt from all those dense woody borders and specimens the hugest of trusses where last spring bloom ran grandest. They won't do it again. Bloom will, however, arise from this year's crop of lusty sprouts, but they need room to mature. I also spend the month severing from steamy thickets branches whose winter damage is irrevocably manifest in August. And then there are all those weighted limbs to be taken down, which were far too heavy to move properly in the returning wind. Or if the wind would not take them low, then ice and snow most surely would.

Early morning is far and away the best time, with dew running from the foliage as a form of most welcome drenching, for one must dress up to this stubborn task, not down—even the least thorny of little shrubs grows defensively armed. My sleeves go down to the wrist and are held in place with rubber bands. Heavy boots are mandatory too, for I don't know why but bits of glass and flip-top lids seem to collect in the shrub border, as if some malign sort of garden lowlife had continual messy picnics in the dark. I tie a large handkerchief to my neck, although it and all others are often torn off and join in the general litter. And so geared and gloved, I dive to the heart of the shrub for the oldest, nastiest-looking stem I can find. And then work my way out. If I leave too large a stump, I will trim it down later. Naturally there is always a thistle growing mournfully there and a beleaguered something that scoots away, vole or mole or just imagination's whatnot as sweat begins to pour. Weak stems all go, for they are mere sap consumers. Only the most vigorous remain. Like all seemingly insurmountable chores, the pruning is done sooner than I expect, and it is a great pleasure to see the whole fellow move in graceful, unencumbered manner. "Well done" is with space enough to put your head through or for "birds to get through unimpeded," or so the Scottish-English formula goes.

The pressing work also involves lifting and dividing bearded iris, fans cut back to six inches, rhizomes set atop the ground like floating ducks. I do this annually, but every other year can suffice. It is a task I rather enjoy. There is the comfort of knowing that I am making life a bit more difficult for the iris borer as it pursues its woeful progress through fan and into rhizome, where it fattens larvae with destructive appetite. Behind the irises, more or less as nurse plants, while cuttings of arctic willows are consolidating, I transplant an excess of globe thistle and rampant baby's breath, and divisions of that delightful prize of the fields bee balm, which goes with wild and cultivated chicory like jam and muffins. The vegetable garden takes two long rows of garlic cloves, now being the best of times to plant them, for they need strong root growth before frost for a swollen harvest next July. There are innumerable other green matters to be lifted into new arrangements, and all of them need generous soaking, rain or not, dew or not, whether the spot is shaded or not; water, water, and more water is always urgent come fall. Roses are pruned, more pesto is put up, and basil plants are hauled out whole and hung upside down in the hot dry air of the tool shed, this being the easier way to get dried leaves for winter, the other being to strip the branches and put the leaves in wire-bottomed trays, but this involves frequent stirring and shaking to have them evenly dry. My lazy way gives better flavor anyway, for each leaf is still receiving liquid and oil from the stalk. The only occasion for dubiousness is that sometime a spider runs webbing through the bunch.

And where the ground mysteriously swales on the meadow lawn I have been sowing grass, mixing the seed in a wheelbarrow with old manure, doing a double task of filling holes as well as reseeding.

And I have been on a fruitless search for native white rhododendron (the *maximus*), this glorious American now almost impossible to acquire container-grown, its place having been taken over by hybrid English vulgarities whose annual eruptions seem to announce Mother's Day for a month and a half. These days, this calm, persuasive aristocrat of our woods is wrenched wild from North Carolina's slopes by gatherers who work the hills only in the spring. It comes to us high risk in burlap but worth it. In bloom or not, it gives half-lit areas indigenous swank. It and the mountain laurel are what we mean when we say "an American wild garden."

Planting Bulbs

I DO LIKE to get bulbs in early, partly for them, partly for me, partly because a bulb with a lot of smart root growth will have a finer purchase on winter, but mostly because kneeling on dark, damp, cold, late October earth with the wind blowing, hands slathered in mud, shoes to be left outside the door, pants straight to the laundry, is a rotten way of ending the planting year and an excellent way to undermine winter equilibrium.

I have ordered *Crocus susianus* (also sold as *C. angustifolius*), an early bunch-flowered crocus striped brown over summer butter-yellow, for planting in turf and under cedars. I think I will ease the tedium by use of a metal spike and sledgehammer and simply poke holes, sift a bit of bone meal in the base, and cover with a mixing of good earth and peat moss mixed ready in a wheelbarrow. In spreads or drifts. I have ordered several thousand. I will toss them up and to the side, and where they fall they will go in. If one is leery about cropping bulb foliage on the lawn before the leaves mature and the lawn begins to look like ripe cover crop, I would recommend crocuses, snowdrops, snowflakes, and the earliest species daffodils rather than the trumpets, which bloom later and may stay foliate through June. Tiny as these bulbs may be, in masses on a lawn just greening they are splendid.

I will not make holes but yank strips of turf and then plant and roll the strip back. Single white *Galanthus elwesii* is a wonderfully snowy snowdrop, but I prefer bolder introductions on lawns and think snowflakes are better. *Leucojum vernum,* the spring snowflake, which is white tipped green, hints vaguely at the cup of a mountain laurel flattened out and simplified. I went to tulips in the catalogue for replacements for those that finally either wore out or were inadvertently sliced by my trowel as I was moving this or that. I have ordered *praestans* 'Fusilier', an incomparable tulip.

I pay little heed to recommended depths, for one must make continual accommodations to one's own soils. If an area of soil strikes me as being of light weight and consistency, the bulbs go deeper. Where peculiar pockets of heavy earth seem to swell up in groundswell bulges suggesting huge frost pressures, the bulbs are closer to the surface. But this may be of no ultimate matter. Bulbs travel up and they travel down with marvelous alacrity, adapting to soil weight within a year. Under a *Magnolia stellata,* daffodils I planted years ago bunch just below the surface and seem content to be at such perilous level and continue doing well. Elsewhere, the same autumn contingent struck deeper, deeper in sandier soil and generally in more open spaces, where protection seems paramount.

Spring bulbs are welcome anywhere, but some situations will suit their resurrected grace in greatly heightened degree. Through goldenrod and tansy stalk rubble, the simple snowdrop is a thing of greater promise than an expected wash in the main flowerbed. Under an outside step

I have dogtooth violets and next to them on the pebbles frail hooped daffodils, which replace *Iris reticulata,* eager puffs of yellow or blue seemingly without stem. Early bulbs go in darkest or brightest location; the middle areas of light do quite well with rushes or perennial foliage, pale and lovely as any blossom. Although I am lavish with bulbs, I stick to the overriding rule that anything added to the garden's collection must be high in performance and durability. Once these various colonies take hold, wanderers increase the pleasure, explorers straight from the center of the clump, heaved up by frost and rolled in the wind as minute bulbs.

Daffodils are indispensable components of the natural garden. If properly planted, they need not ever be lifted. They multiply, but discreetly, and if one avoids the newest sensations are entirely in the realm of the affordable. They swank on year after year in rock gardens, through meadow or lawn, under trees or understory bushes, and are stunning above a mulch of pebbles. Daffodils can be everywhere and have no capacity to overwhelm, for their abundance has a certain Episcopal sobriety. Through winter straw and duff, their stubborn yet insouciant courage comes through without shrillness. They are the perfect endorsement of spring.

Plant the trumpet varieties as you would sow grass, with large gestures from the shoulder, in sweeps. Imitate the scarf flung on an entry table and you will have it. Practice this empty-handed until you have got it down cold and then walk where you think you would like to see them this spring and many springs to come. Then order a bushel and sow them in earnest. A side bag tied to the waist will hold enough for a few good throws. Plant each bulb where it falls.

The secret of permanent naturalizing is to plant each

bulb an inch deeper than is recommended and with plenty of slow-dissolving bone meal for adequate future nutrition. Deeper planting seems to be the clue to forestall eventual crowding, all such bulbs being sensitive to excessive warmth, which warmth induces splitting and which splitting will give you a stand of daffodil grass and not bloom. Even so, a year or two of such thin foliage and you will find that some bulbs will mature into bloomers again and then the great gold effect will return as before. I have had this experience with tulips as well, a stand of which I have not lifted for over a dozen years. A year or two will be skimpy or bloomless and then stalwart flowers return, increased. All my bulbs have been behaving so. They are all botanical snaps.

The one persistent difficulty is the long requisite time for their foliage to mature. Nourishment for future bulbs is set in their leaves. The mandate has always been never to cut leaves down until they have withered naturally, but few gardens can stand this unsightly affair. If the spring has been adequately warm and wet and growth has been steady in its urgency, I prefer a general thumb-rule of allowing four or five weeks for maturation and then I lop the foliage at ground level; I have never ruined the future crop. If the leaves are masked by other leaves, I let them do as they wish, but if they are in positions that are too prominent, I follow the former regime. If the spring has been dry or otherwise inclement, all bulbs are allowed to mature according to their own mechanism.

Striking Vegetables

It is never more autumn than when I strike the vegetable garden. The whole theater of it goes. The feeling gets under way that life is going to be one deep cello, its mood dark brown, the melody growing faint. Last Tuesday I lifted bamboo stakes from still-bearing pole beans, and their ungraceful sprawls were then easily pulled. Late beans are funny beans, flesh a bit gelid, fine-looking but not very palatable. All blooming shoots were cropped from the tomatoes on their trellises (these are permanent), the better to make green fruits swell and ripen. The leeks were hilled for easier digging this winter. Later they will be heavily mulched. Various bright green Chinese celeries and cabbages and boiling greens that I forgot to plant less of went, regrettably, on the pile. Pods fell on fruit, half-full sacks of this and of that. Vegetables that one cooks, vegetables that one eats raw, slicing vegetables. Stalk, root, and fruit. The immature, the withered, and the still prosperous, the sap-drained and the plump, in bloom or budding. The whole promising mass tromped down for convenient lifting and then toted to ground-hugging shrubs for composting underneath their natural screens—such messes when decaying ought to be hidden. Just about everything green is a suitable mulch in situ, except stuff from the edible part of the garden.

Food factory that that garden is, it is also pablum for bugs. Whatever insects have lived and fed in it have also laid spawn for future generations. Malevolent viral strains too are incorporated in stalk and root. All of it must be cleared. I comb the ground not once but several times with a light bamboo rake and try to remove the smallest leaf and twig. And then I sow annual rye. It is now sprouted. On top of it will go many barrows of manure. Winter months will be a kind of leaven for the grass and the manure and the hay (for salt hay will be spread too)—the cold and the freezing and the thawing a sort of enzyme, catalyzing the fibers, breaking the manure, and making the whole layered structure available for nutrition in spring, when the soil will be deeply turned and all go under.

I did save the trunks of the basil for scented kindling. Rows of red-skinned garlic went in at the end of August, and the peas I planted then are already bearing, sweeter to me than those of June. I have late sowings of beets, white turnips, globe and cylindrical Japanese radishes. The small patch at the back of the garden where I toss flats of seeds that don't sprout is now full of peculiar and tardy germinators. A rambunctious and grateful grass palm is one I'll pot for a friend. But the gray, mitteny English mulleins I'll have to leave, as they are impossible to transplant. That's all right, though. They will be quite heroic there next summer, and I'll double up the planting in some other space to make up for the area lost. Chervil, that impish mixture of licorice and tarragon, has once again been errant and undependable, sprouting now with an almost self-sown abundance. Under mulching, it will winter through and do quite nicely next spring, when its tricks will start again. It is an annual with biennial ways and it will grow where it wants to, like bells of Ireland or dill. All soils and culture are the same to it, except that once it is in a garden it will take care of itself, self-sowing, a bit milder in taste each succeeding generation, growing precisely where you don't want it. It's with the *fraises des bois* this year. My winter spinach has bolted, although nights were quite cool. Vegetables can be more quixotic than flowers, but then, we ask far more of them.

Although I began striking the vegetable beds earlier than usual, I have been doing it so slowly, a row or part of it at a time, that I am still not done, still hunting for clues to the poor performance of some, the better of others. I must not blame everything on the weather but continue the hunt for finer, tougher varieties. While considering these, I find that I may have to take out the lining of chives that runs on the left sides of the two oblique crossed paths. It is an awfully messy, slippery chore to clip chives back several times during the growing season to keep them from getting tan and withery. The time spent might be better put elsewhere. But I do like their blooms very much. If I move them, I may put some in the blue border or a single long ribbon somewhere else. Chives look better, I think, in a line than in a mass, for the umbels arch in a natural skelter and ought to be allowed the space to do so. If I lift them, I will then plant *fraises des bois* on the other side, so that both paths will be lined with them on both sides and then all stepping will be easier. Chives drag their green lines. It is as hard to keep them tidy as it is to get those final strands of pasta on a plate already full.

Next season I will be planting 'Tokyo Cross' turnips again. A late sowing of these white turnips came up surprisingly well, with fat, glistening roots entirely free of eelworm and canker. While not as good as 'Blanc des Navets Marteaux' for grating, they are sufficiently mild to be eaten raw when young and lightly cooked when larger. The 'Marteaux' come down with just about everything and only one in three comes up clean. Foliage to root, 'Tokyo Cross' is a very fine hybrid.

As for the spinach I planted at the same time, well, it didn't. A winter variety whose name eludes me at the moment. But I am coming to think that spinach is at best a fumble. One needs so very much of it to get a serving. The puffed leaf structure collapses under heat. Raw, however, it does balloon up a salad bowl. Spinach, to my way of thinking, is a vegetable that takes very well to commercial canning. Forget what you know about it fresh and taste the tinned product. Not spinach. Not really green, but a different vegetable with a new and rather nice flavor. I think it is fine for a cold winter salad, fussed a bit with lemon and pepper, garlic and oil. So why grow this finicky fellow at all?

I still have parsnips and will be mulching them for the winter. With high foliage and a long taproot, they seem not to have been affected by the June deluges. I would have expected celeriac, for much the same reasons, to have fared as well, but its roots are smaller and more gnarled than last year's, and although it is still quite flavorful for rémoulade, its shape makes grating difficult.

Celery, its cousin in kind, has thinner stalks than last

year, a bit stringy in its outside, but I am getting some fine centers. Leeks are meager and small. The various parsleys I planted all did well, and I have potted a few for the winter window.

Bell peppers fruited but stayed on the small side and had to be planted twice, as the first set got thick-stemmed from the cold and wouldn't respond to later warmth. But at the same time I put out chili peppers, and these went along unaffected by the cold spring and the wet June. I have just picked whole plants to hang upside down to dry and redden; I used some of their green fruit in tomato sauce, an addition that works very well.

If I have been putting tomatoes to the side, it is because their performance was abominable this year. They too were planted twice, but didn't bear ripe fruit until the end of August, fruit with a low flavor and no polish that never made it as sandwich or salad material but had to be put up for sauce. The plum tomatoes had little juice in their vessels, the slicing tomatoes too much meal. I have green fruit for later ripening (stem down, wrapped in newspaper at about fifty degrees) but not as many as I should, as most are marked, and marked tomatoes rot instead of ripen.

Squash did well, but squash is not an indicator of very much, if planted out when the soil is warm. The two new rows of asparagus I set out have come into the fall robust and I should have first pickings the spring after next. And three staggered plantings of beets were fine. But everything this year is couched in a *but*. The patch has been no pleasure. Beets leafed too much and the roots were on the small side and seemed not as sweet as I would like them to be. Should this happen next year, I will see about cutting off much of the foliage in order to plump them up.

PLANT PORTRAITS VI

Helenium

ALMOST UNIQUE in all its mostly awkward ways, helenium is the great advertiser of autumn. Mine begins blooming at the end of August and continues for some time through September. If I deadhead the blooms, lateral issues will supply trusses in October as well. It is exactly the sort of random, dusty field signature to assert and develop the theme of fruiting and ripening. But it looks as if the transition from field to garden has a little undone it, and pausing midway, it got stuck on a pile left by a developer.

Helenium is a plant seemingly of the open lot, a little bit of this and rather too much of that. It has a nice flat top of daisylike blooms, but unevenly flat and with an impudent raised loaf of a button for each center, very much like that of a black-eyed Susan with yeast in it. With its wild, unkempt look, it is best at the back borders, where its gawkiness can tumble about. It is a favorite of Europeans but not Americans. This is a great pity, for if we did invest interest in it, hybridizers might go after its problems and lay off roses and daylilies, which are rapidly turning into horticultural lapdogs.

If you like blossoms of the dust, helenium is for you. Sneezeweed is its common name. It likes full sun and rich or poor soil, and that is that. Stake if you have a mind to, or not; it is all the same to this terrifically hardy perennial, which at the stake will still manage to avoid looking kempt. It is immune to just about all diseases, except sometimes aphids will attack the roots and then you must lift the plant and wash off the soil and place it somewhere else. I've never had any trouble with mine. If the wind takes the stems down, the flowers hang on, still attracting bees.

What is so striking about helenium is its wonderfully sooty soft petals. In the varieties available to Americans, the brown and the yellow, the first looks as if it were sprinkled with cinnamon, the second with curry. But what lies underneath is the real treat, a damasking of color not immediately apparent in the busy sociability of the summer border, but one that gets stuck in the eye and is a relief when all other flash begins to pall.

Sneezeweeds are perfect for the wild garden or what we call a meadow garden—the hardest of all gardens to grow with any degree of substantial repetition and reward, except the one of inadvertence and hazard. You get what comes into the meadow garden, that's for sure, but seldom what you want. What you plant may be erased forever from the spot where you put it, or seedlings of it may land unnoticed by you but always elsewhere. A bed of helenium surrounded by that ghastly green plastic lawn edger sunk below the soil surface might protect the garden from invasion, but it might also contain the plant's vigor to the extent that it chokes itself out without the relief of annual division.

I don't care much for the bother of lifting and splitting, however, and I do so only when a group looks extremely uncomfortable. Some years, therefore, my helenium looks a little starved, but that's an acceptable mien for a plant used to fending for itself. What we like in green growth beyond the garden hedge is endurance, and helenium has it in plenty.

Helenium is not, by the way, Helen's flower at all, I find. Or, for that matter, the flower of Helenus, who was the son of Priam. It seems that although it is from the Greek, it is from the Greek name for something else originally named for Helen of Troy. But when I think of Helen, I do think of someone incredibly brown and gold.

Cosmos

In the middle of high autumn, minor frosts end; hard black ones begin. Except for the raring of wild birds in from the sea, breaking periods of rest, all motion at the tail of the growing season is down. Finished production rains. Berries go down, and so too leaves, seeds, and sap. Although there are still flowers, they have been felted by frost and marked by slowed, niggardly nutrition. Days are short. And as welcome as any flowers may be, they are but chancy stragglers and holdouts. Down, down. Things are over. Year after year, however, and just at this time, I find a single clump of white cosmos somewhere in the garden, entirely untouched by it all.

Cosmos is a flower born for the vases of roadside stands and more graceful there perhaps than in the garden, but most gardeners will put it in in masses, and therein is the disappointment, for it is rather derelict of behavior. It is quite a mess, with a readiness to flop or hold back its floral production if it is too well fed. Even mild storms will break it. It will crack under the most ordinary of heavy summer rain, and a bed of such fallen stuff is too difficult to mend. As an easy sprouter and a self-sower, it will appear in the most improbable places, and here is where it will perform best and display best, singly and unmassed. I have grown it hot out of the base of a rough fieldstone wall and at random in a bed of something else. I even like it when it doesn't flower, but this is a queer personal taste, for most garden writers do not like its thinness and lack of density. It is foliage in thinnest strips, rather like something chiffonaded for the pot, and I find that its green wiriness is rather like wettened fur or feathers or dry eyelashes firmly curled.

In ordinary seasons, cosmos will suffer in August and revive in autumn and be done in by severity, but every year I find a single clump surviving the wildest sort of storms, and I am not surprised really to have a post-hurricane survivor. It is sometimes listed as a tender perennial, and the species themselves, both annual and perennial, are native to Mexico and Bolivia, probably deriving hardihood from the reinforcing nights of the *alto plano*.

The white that I have is from a variety called, I believe, 'Purity'. I am not sure, though, for I have saved seeds from it year after year, the color being seldom pushed in the catalogues, and I may have forgotten its patented name. White is generally now available only in mixtures, which is the pits. In Burpee, Stokes, and Harris, the three catalogues nearest to hand, I find instead a listing for 'Diablo'. It is described as a "brilliant fiery red." What, I wonder, can one ever place next to it? Then there is (oh, come now) 'Pinkie', and something I take to be very useful when one is lost in an Alaskan night called 'Early Klondyke Orange Flare'. This Klondyke (Harris catalogue spelling) is a type that is denser of leaf. Its broad foliage looks to me more like Italian parsley, and who would want that surmounted by a coreopsis-type flower scald-orange in hue? Carrots will do for that kind of parsley, and that is that. Breeders have not only raised the heat of cosmos color (in a white laboratory, I suppose, any color is welcome) and unnecessarily lengthened the petal but have gone on to further wrack by working at doubles and so far are giving us big, hot, salad-plate editions called "crested," with half-curled cabbage strands poked on top. Breeders, alas, also work out in the fields, where the rainbow has fallen and only oddness seems to stand out.

The loveliness of cosmos rests in its unassuming commonness. Breeders are not gardeners, and neither, it seems, are seed catalogue writers, for again and again the advice is to mass the cosmos—which is why they continue to disappoint. If cosmos must be put in so chancy a situation as a mass, then why not between things broad and shrubby—or behind, for when they fall (as always they will, even the recent 'Bush' variety), a nice strong branch will insinuate itself through massed foliage in front to seek the sun, and there it will emerge wonderfully.

The name is Greek and refers to the beauty of symmetry, with all that it intimates of order and perfection. In the universe, even marred things find their place in heaven (fallen foliage rotting, turning to soil, rising once again as nutrition). So too the cosmos downed by storms, some of whose branches do not die but root again.

The plant blooms on and on in the inner garden,

although the place is now dark for more hours than it is light. Even as the days rapidly shorten and the gray of everything stains and spreads, the whiteness of the continually unfolding blooms is stronger and stronger. Beneath it, autumn crocuses mauved violet by saffron dabs of pollen lie low, open at noon, shut by three.

Milkweed

I am not sure now whether it was I or my young cousins who made them each late summer and early autumn, but I vividly recall those bright, clumsy, fabulous birds constructed of green, unsplit milkweed pods. The eyes were buttons sewn at the neck end, through the sides on one knotted thread if you were thick-fingered and exactly level on two light stitches flush at either side if you were adept. The legs were of pipe cleaners poked gently through the plump base, and sometimes were colored. It was always hard to make them stand, so we often despaired of trying and simply socked them all together in nests made of scraps of wrapping paper, as if they were fledglings. I cannot recall, however, whether we went so far as to attempt bills and wings, for we were a silent, intense little group who took to projects rather grudgingly but then got deep about them.

"Why, those are my Caracas balls grown up," I recall my grandmother saying, for she had been at milkweed too, in its earlier flowering state. A large bowl of her dried collections, shellacked and often hideously colored, stood on a table in front of the pier glass in the hall, and with smaller variations sometimes in some upstairs bedroom. These were mummies from the huge bouquet of fresh anything (so long as it was loose and wild) that got added to on the open porch throughout the summer.

Milkweed is a very American plant, *Asclepias* the milkweed, but its bold symmetries mixed with quirky asymmetries, its onionlike flower blooming in clefts made by the leaves along the stem (but not all the way), its large seedpod utterly unlike what one would expect such roundness to produce, its young shoots near to those of peony or rhubarb, and as lusty but paler, make for a sort of oriental impression. (I could see it, just visible on the far side of a moon gate in a garden in Souchow, its sturdy umbels tucked in the simple ovate leaves as ready for brush and ink as any bamboo.) Its demeanor is fresh and young yet portly and a bit grave, as if it were aware of its complicated gifts. The daylily, the daisy, the chicory, and the milkweed make for one of the most entirely satisfying natural combinations in the summer meadow, yet I have never been able to choose between it alone, in single example, or massed by itself with a few pioneers drifting off into erasings of ripening timothy. It is of an enormous family, some two thousand species of perennials and climbing shrubs, and although most of them are African, the few we have seem utterly American. They are so vigorous that they fooled Linnaeus, who seems not to have been aware that the type he was studying had been introduced to Europe from America just before 1629. He called it Syriaca, and it carries this name, *Asclepias syriaca*, out in our fields and I suppose does have a bit of Ali Baba about it.

The family is named for Aesculapius, god of medicine, shown by the ancients with Hygeia, goddess of wise living, on one side and Panakeia, goddess of cure-alls, on the other. Milkweed was born for patent medicines. The seed, boiled or soaked in a little water, was used to draw poison from snakebites. Early settlers used the sap to remove warts and corns and calluses. Boiled and applied in solution, it was said to dissolve headaches and, one might suppose, the skin of the head as well. On and on the prescriptives go. The root was used as an emetic, a diuretic, an anthelmintic, and a general stomachic. Mrs. Grieves writes that it "strengthens the heart in the same way as digitalis and is a quick and certain diuretic. It is given in dropsy as a diuretic in place of digitalis, also in coughs, colds, rheumatism from cold, threatened inflammation of the lungs. Also in diarrhoea, gastric catarrh, certain skin eruptions of an erysipelatous nature and in asthma and dyspnoea. It acts as a vermifuge . . ." No mention, however, is made in any recent work of the floss or kapok that stuffed life preservers in World War II, those bulging, bulky jackets called by airmen Mae Wests—and I hear that milkweed was spun in the eighteenth century into a very lovely, cottonlike material too fragile for use, owing to the shortness of the thread and, even when mixed with real cotton, its weakness.

Use of the milkweed, like that of any well-examined plant, drifted toward the table as well. Indians used pods, leaves, and shoots. Blossoms and buds were flavorers and thickeners. Canadian French prepared the tender spring shoots like asparagus. I've tried it. It's good. Sturtevant tells us in *Edible Plants of the World* that the flowers made "a very good, brown, palatable sugar . . . These are shaken early in the morning before the dew is off them when there falls from them with the dew a kind of honey, which is reduced into sugar by boiling." The plant has a quite fabulous odor. The perfume of its blooms on a hot, windless day in July is like lilacs or roses or both and a breathtaking something else, the sweet continent of its enlarged root perhaps close to iris or lilies or the smell of America, the odor of our invisible inheritance. It seems the very worth of our laws, the silent agreement we have made to obey, the way we believe in reciprocal courtesies. It takes me to the earth of my childhood.

The *Revised Dictionary* of the Royal Horticultural Society is appreciative of the milkweed's garden qualities and describes it as a "handsome border plant . . . thriving in peaty or light rich soil, increased by division in spring and sometimes [sometimes, indeed!] by seeds." It has been in every garden I have had, a wild member of the community of plants that comes ever closer to my borders as if it were either curious or lazy or reticent, always there but not particularly intrusive. It still waits at the edges and perhaps always will, for I prefer to see it in a more or less tangential position. It doesn't quite finish up well by being tamed and seems a bit reduced in vigor, like clumps of daisies, which are always better in meadows.

Japanese Wood Anemone

The flowers and fruits of autumn are grand courtly members of the plant kingdom. With little time to spare, like the coda at the end of the symphony, they repeat with great brevity all the energy and color spent previously in leisurely development and proliferation. The pale pink rose is pinker near frost, hugeness reigns in the apple world, grapes are swamped by heavy sugars, stalks are thick middle-aged affairs, and the bassoon, not the violin, might play for pumpkins, squash, and turnips. Through the myriad greens run layers of brown and gold. Something is departing, yes, but with an exit rounded and full. And then the Japanese wood anemone begins to bloom, exactly as if it were spring.

If one wants to do its name properly, and be Latin about it, one strikes the third vowel, but the second will suffice for ordinary use, if you can pronounce it at all. If not, windflower will do. Anemos, the wind, sent his namesakes, the anemones, to herald spring. It seems the Japanese wood anemone loitered long in order to make a single, spectacular late entrance. He is a brancher, from a plant soft and downy with shortish hairs, on two- to five-foot stems that are wiry and dark and appear invisible when masked by other foliage. At the ends are simple, translucent flowers like the first simple openers of April. They are not immediately noticeable at first in a garden border soaked in strong color, and they may appear to be but specks of frost-colored foliage or petals stripped from other blooms caught floating in the tepid air. But once the eye has centered on the pale and insubstantial April hues, the wood anemone becomes pivotal, and when planted against a holly or allowed to stray through mountain laurel brings admiration back to them as well. It comes in several shadows of pink and white and rosy and an almost mauve, but flushed is a better name for its spectrum.

With all its need for being shielded against the very thing it signifies—the wind—it is nevertheless a tough fellow and should be grown more. And it ought to go in the mixed and tall border, or against walls, or under shrubs or surrounded by them, or set apart if it is sheltered above a plat of bricks, so that the plant, basal leaf and candelabra stem, can be admired entire. Any good garden soil will do, with a mixing of some sand seemingly helpful. That, and ample moisture and full sun or partial shade, and there you are. Plant the anemones in generous clumps and then let them alone. They never need lifting or dividing.

The difficult thing is to acquire specimens. Mine I grew from seed I got in England, I think, or was it plants from Wayside Gardens? I cannot recall at the moment. I do remember a splendid stand in the back of a local nursery, but they were not for sale. If we all ask for them, nurseries will carry them. There are some semidoubles in white, but I consider them a breeder's vulgarism, for the flowers have too much weight and their whole point is blitheness. They bloom, by the way, from September through quite late frosts, when withering and dying get so large in our eyes.

Anemone's other tale is that it is the tears of Venus, who weeps and laments as she wanders distractedly through the forest for the golden one, Adonis.

Transplanting

AUTUMNS PASS BY too quickly to be recollected much. I am so busy, I cannot recall whether we had much of a period of sustained warmth following killing frost last year, which is the time of true Indian summer. I do know, however, that foliage this year is in extraordinarily fine peak and that this has been rare for many years, a type of display eastern Long Island is apparently not quite north enough for, lacking strong dips in night temperatures and clear, stubbornly clear skies. Overnight a young *Acer griseum* (a maple whose bark peels) flamed out from its slender trunk, leaves outlined in suspension against dark cedars. Even those cedars, whose older needles annually send down a most pleasing wrapping-paper hue, suggest fruition rather than death. Even withered privet leaves are agreeable, not tatty. On grass gone blue in the morning mist, their curled leafage is as dark and light as dark and light tobacco, or the burl and stem of a pipe well smoked. I wish I had more time for pausing, more time to stare.

I have been on my knees mostly, lifting mulches from two large beds where wild sorrel has all too vehemently taken hold. It must be removed with enormous caution because the roots, as orange and as viable as those of bittersweet, break easily, throwing sendups in a bed one thinks one has thoroughly cleaned. As I thought, before I put down the mulch. A very nasty weed. It likes nothing better than to romp through clumps of daylilies and Siberian iris, thread through bee balm, and attempt to emulate, when in heartiest flush, the foliage of cultivated chicory. I would sooner separate and plant an acre of leeks than go through this task again, and I have no one to blame but myself for thinking that the plants would be easier to get rid of when matted together, so that they could be taken up rather like a sheet of paper. And I have more, much more to pull.

But it has been the loveliest autumn. I have never seen such yellows. Overnight, when the ginkgoes went up into their legendary yellow, the one to the south first and then the one to the north, both joined the clethra, the *Rosa glauca,* and bright skeletons of asparagus plumes, all so golden that they were distinct at night, moon or not. Even a single daylily is popping out, it too yellow.

I don't know whether I have been right or not, there being no truly unbreakable rules in gardening. As in painting, one manipulates a very few rather general, unspecific concepts or procedures and does not hew to an orderly list of commandments. Interpretation is the painter's and the gardener's way of life, and as much as I am leery of autumn transplanting and often advise against it, I have been doing a lot of it. When I do transplant, I transplant so quickly, I would prefer to call it a system of rearrangement. Holes are dug for each and every candidate, and each and every one is singly lifted and put in new disposition without a wait. No part of the precious root hairs is allowed to dry. I do this in the late afternoon and then soak, often by flashlight.

As for the holes, they are dug several days in advance and the soil is liberally mixed with peat moss, turned and turned again, and watered thoroughly several times. When it can be poured through the hand, clodless and thoroughly and evenly moist, top of hole to bottom of hole, the plant is lifted and set. It too has been prepared several days in advance, the earth around it pulled free of entanglement, the proper digging tools ready and on site before the job is begun. And this includes the wheelbarrow. In no wise do I neglect several soakings beforehand. A major undertaking. The ride in the wheelbarrow must be smooth. All one's doing will be fruitless if the passage is bumpy. I have areas with large and difficult pebbles. These stretches get boards down as tracks for the carting.

Manuring

THE MICE AND I have been industrious—they indoors out of the autumn, and I spreading manure outdoors in the wet and cold. Forty-five wheelbarrows equal one truck, more or less, the number hanging on the holding capacity of the wheelbarrow, the consistency, age, and dryness of the pile. Someone asked me whether I count the loads, thereby giving me a large clue as to how to stall the monotony . . . I have, according to such tally, loaded and carted and spread 180 full wheelbarrows and have 45 more to go. It is definitely down work, although not especially heavy or unpleasant, the manure being horse stabling mixed with bedding straw, easy to load, easy to spread. And it is a nice darkish cinnamon, vaguely ammoniac, good to look at, heady to sniff.

The thump of the shovel on the wooden barrow's side is a serious sound, not at all sad. But nothing at all relieves this simple tedium, this low work with one's eyes grounded when autumn haze is so fine. The smallest swell on the levelest track has alpine ambitions, while its other side becomes a runway into pits. Vines catch at the tire and wind around it. Corners must be taken at the proper speed. At each location, the cart must be tipped, and a good shovelful and a half can never be scraped out. And then there are things other than manure in the pile.

We drink a lot in stables, it seems, and sometimes bottles break. Life there is as careless as it is full of pints. We write notes too, with stubby pencils and ancient pens, and we receive letters. Envelopes emerge with almost readable addresses, writ large and hard by hands to whom writing is an unaccustomed act. And then there is raveling. Blue cotton threads one year, orange the next, twines of various hues emerging, catching on shrubs, seeming like blossoms or the work of spiders on hallucinogens. My manure must come from a show stable, for these are the braidings of manes and tails when mounts are groomed for meets. Which solves the mystery of the colored threads but not the misery of the drinkers in the barn and whether their letters held bad news.

Piles are often very far from where they belong in the garden, access for the truck being limited. I have a double pile near the main flower garden, one for general shrub culture, one near the vegetable garden, and one for the blueberries. Perhaps I ought to count steps or shovelfuls, how many to each load, and multiply the whole lot to keep my head going, but any work done over and over is better done dumb.

Manure is the pump at the heart of a good garden. Where it goes annually is everywhere, of course, but in greatly varying amounts. With mulch as a side dividend of the straw, composting is unnecessary. I give most to what has grown most, flowered most, fruited most. Daylilies mat down to their own nourishment and so get just a dressing, but roses and asparagus, whose foliage will do them no good, whose flowers have sapped strength, and whose stalks have landed in the cooking pot—they are heaped high. Young hedges to make great growth, shrubs overstoried by trees, berries, of course, and grapes need much. And then there is that fine control of future height. Where one shrub, for reasons of its own, has prospered far more than its neighbor, the poor show gets more. In this way, next year's balance will be gained. Where peat moss has been laid on rhododendron and mountain laurel, manure goes on top to stall winter blowing. Plants in pebbled areas get enough to be fed but not enough to drown the pebbles. Where foliage is dense, the shovelful is pitched on its furnishings and wind and rain will sift it all through. For a good foot on either side, paths are kept clear, for the dressing will spread and anything closer would require continual sweeping. Scotch thistles and mullein get none. They need none. Oldest trees are on their own management, except those with exceptionally filching roots, which get enough to keep the wandering slow. Peonies only a light top dressing all on the side and none on the crowns, for peonies can't stand weight and won't bloom if they are burdened. Where wild lilies have come through brush, they too are fed, as are spring bulbs of the more diminutive sort, the ones closest to the surface. Deeper bulbs can be skipped, having been laid with liberal amounts of bone meal, and they have a way, or so it seems to me, of participating in the more generalized fertility of the garden, undoubtedly from winter washings and spring rains. The meadow grass is left alone, for I take nothing from it and when it is cut, the mowing stays.

A good week's work, and then a cat for the mice.

November Blooms

I HAVE BEEN TAKING my annual late November tally of nonquitters, flowers that don't stop. Ten years of this, and if I can conclude anything at all about their performance, it is that it has nothing whatever to do with the weather and everything to do with genetic good fortune, which, were it translated into our own stunning selves, we might honor by calling determination or courage. Herbal lustiness is similarly only a trait of the generous few. Or are they profligate? I wonder. Sort of grasshoppers, as opposed to ants. I am not just noting greenness of gardens, for the greenness of the hills is more durable than understandable and true bareness something one wakes to with rather a surprise around about the middle of next month. This flowering of indestructibles in late November gives pause, whether the season be mild or not, wet or dry, blustery or calm. Flowers difficult to spot at first because one simply doesn't expect to see them.

I did have a theory about ground heat based on dwarf snapdragon behavior, for it seemed to me that the lowest flowers performed longest. Then I realized that for several years I had been looking low, as if hunting for something that wouldn't be there, when the roses were still out on the railings (as were the most rampant clematis, higher up still). If you don't want to see something, it is clear that you won't, which is why people who are unhappy remain so; a physically diminished sphere of vision goes with depression like any fixed idea looking for reinforcement. All that one has to do is to say that spring is here to note a randomness in leg, arm, and hand movements, while saying *winter* suddenly will get to the limbs like frost. Autumn is the season when one persistently maintains that there will never be another perfect day like the one just over, just as persistently forgetting that one has said so frequently the whole of the season.

Here they are still, the flowers. Roses, the flower we think about when we think of love. Many lonely gardeners grow them. I found 'Blanc Double de Coubert' by tracking its scent. It stays. In autumn it stays longer and it is crisper. It was in the middle of one newly opened flower and busily budding several others. And farther on, 'Goldbusch' on the dog pen, with brawny pointed buds in quantity and two two-day-old blooms. And that thing of things, 'Climbing American Beauty', of disgustingly high color that I insist on having one of. It is a red that black-and-white catalogues of roses suddenly stain their advertisements with when they want to knock a customer flat. It is a red that nowhere fits but demands and gets a wall or an arbor and much attention and I guess deserves it. It does rather seem to tie the garden together, however, like a good-luck ribbon on a plant in the window of a new laundromat. Nothing finishes off exalted cuisine like a bowl of anything so long as it has chocolate in it.

Again the 'Duchess of Edinburgh' decided to put on her glorious old Edwardian hat to show the rest of the garden that royals are born to endure discomfort and consider weather of any sort a form of impertinence. The dear old thing chose to ignore a 'Jackmanii', latecomer to the clan *Clematis.* It was doing the very same thing around the corner, albeit in front of and not behind a railing. Shasta daisies cut down were coming up again, brighter and whiter (if a bit shorter) in the clear cold air. And chamomile thick and chamomile thin and garlic chives for the third time this season. Out beyond the hedge a favorite lemon daylily and a few daisies naturalized and a white campion. And did I see a pink? I almost think so.

Hard to find, all of them, as I have said, in the way that one doesn't notice the fineness of furniture when it is covered up for the winter, even though the covers might have slipped. So I made a tour twice before I realized that blue lobelias were still out with more coming and that the leeks had been purpled by frost and were glorious, so that those that I lay out among the flowers for blooming purposes give additional dividends—I must remember this and put them perhaps against something dark. I had quite passed by the 'Old China Monthly', the one flower expected to continue, because by then I was looking more up and sideways than down. It was not only blooming, it was growing more branches. But I have picked it in the third week of December. Easier now with my eyes, I found new tansy among the old, copper mums continuing to bud, and old English pinks and the weeping crab, 'Red Jade', decked with more ruby fruits than ever it had had. But I must confess to being tired of flowers. I am of a winter mind now and much more kin to strawy goldenrod downed by the wind and all the neutral twigs and branches that will take the amazing light of the coming months.

It is not a dying at all. It is a small reprise of the tune, running through the thinning air, each time the furious sunsets of November gather, each time the earth drains to the color of bone. One of the great gifts to the Northeast gardener is that color, as he knows it, eventually will go and be replaced by color he must accept as having weight and utility too.

And then there was this single blue violet.

Birds

I THINK I may put down the rumor I have come across several times that feeding birds domesticates them. I have never known a bird to go for dried nuts when a worm (or a raspberry, for that matter) is around. Feeding birds is saving them from starvation. Feeding them is keeping them in the garden, where they will repay one's efforts with handsome inroads on the insect population, and the theft of fruit or berry is small loss compared to this gain. I do not say pamper them, that the beak of the finch, because of its shape, is incapable of taking anything other than expensive thistle seed. Chick-cracked corn in hundred-pound sacks is all that they get during the winter and for as long as the cold weather lasts in autumn and spring. Corn is total nutrition and satisfies all birds when they are hungry, from junco to cardinal and mourning dove to even the rare brown thrasher. Invasions of junk birds don't last very long. They are called junk because they are so obstreperous and so numerous, but the habits and looks of occasional starlings and grackles do have intrinsic allure.

Birds are unsentimental fellows, very rude to one

another and peckers all. I have seen a hawk make its kill right from one of the three feeders near the window (these stations are rectangles of wood on posts with two screened holes for drainage and four sides of wood stripping to keep the feed from blowing) and drag it down to the ground as others returned to feed, the killer being safely occupied. One of the side benefits of chick-cracked corn in its inexpensive bulk amounts is that being cracked, it doesn't germinate. And mixed birdseed is full of seed one doesn't want in the garden, and squirrels generally ignore cracked corn, preferring the whole. Mice like it, but they like anything. For them there is the owl that lives in a post near the trash, and he is a fine hunter. Last year I spread over nine hundred pounds of inexpensive corn, and it is grand to have nestings all over the garden.

The Hill

THE BROWN HILL before the south window of the winter studio. The brown hill that I want red. I think of dwarf barberry, but I detest its horrid thorns. They get in the way of its satisfying scarlet fruit. Or a few fine rampant *wichurana* roses high with rosy hips. But the something red I am looking for has to be short, for it will be growing on the hill. It's a low hill, and a vigorous red would give great definition to its middle distance, *middle* being, of course, an overworked term and a highly conjectural one; *middling* might be more accurate, but anything on the hill has got to be low. Red-twigged dogwood might work (although the soil is definitely prone to drying out quickly), or I might lift runners from the *Hydrangea petiolaris* (the only climber in the hydrangea family) and plant them instead, for their bare young twigs are a handsome orange. But they like damp too. I am fond of climbers used as groundcover, like wisteria or any rambler rose. Or clematis, which might take a slope the way it takes a trellis. But then, the soil, in cinnamon again, is all wrong for the task. Which leads me to broom, graceful and sweeping broom, one of the few decent swayers to keep supple in frigid weather. It would, of course, block the view, but not permanently. A good view is best served in sections. The dullness of a huge piece of glass in front of a good view! Then too, it is very hard to concentrate on what one is doing when all nature is putting on her royal quotidian show. My second studio out here had such a glass wall, and I ended up covering it in brown paper, having come down with an acute case of "Sagaponack stare," which led to a worse case of inertia, exceeding in duration and intensity the one I suffered from in a castle on the River Galway. The hill with broom sounds fine. What is a view anyway but a branch against the sky?

While thinking about branches, I went out yesterday and began pruning the pines along the drive. Now, I am sure that black pines self-prune eventually, like all soft woods should, and there is something so fine about a pine branch that even bare of needles it works. But each tree I planted some ten years ago has also been struggling with strangles of bittersweet, and they are consequently in need of much clearing for the sake of their lives. This will give me sad dingy apertures at the base, where trunks have shimmied off their lower boughs, so I think the time has come to consider planting a lower story or perhaps a high floor.

The pines divide the west line of my property from a field soon to sprout houses, so the matter is quite urgent. The problem is that the barrier pines are also on a terrible blow line, where chemicals pile up from the fields and yearly do damage even to the hedgerow matter, so the choice of planting will be difficult. I do like the idea of native rhododendron and mountain laurel (the hybrid pinkish red fellows look overdressed and floppish), but I think they will always look ailing. I may just solve it with truckloads of soil around the base of the pines, slanted in such a way that I could station the laurel and rhododendron on the leeward side, at the base of the hill. It is a comfort to know that one can amend a climate and block a view by just such a method.

When I made the winter studio, excavation detritus remained piled around it, and I smoothed this into a most natural-looking earthen swell with arctic willow at the top and a row of white rhododendrons below. Between the two plantings I have tossed garden debris to prevent erosion, making an area of compost and leaf mold that has now become a perfect woodland tilth. The spot stays cool and windless and quite moist through long dry periods, for the core of the hill husbands wet to such a degree that all of the earth wicks it to the surface. I will plant woodland flowers here, in holes well stirred with added peat moss. In the first garden I ever made, slash from our woods went down on a gravelly hill year after year, its rot and decay making a splendid loam. I planted moccasin flowers and cardinal, trillium and violet, and am told they are still doing well.

But the more I look at winter, the more I have come to enjoy its supreme and inescapable gift: form—naked, unadorned, and magnificent. The infrastructure of tree and bush, the outlines of path and driveway, the swift hit of a roofline against the sky, all of these are stupendous and a relief after so much matty foliage and cover. After all of our doing, it is the bone we are after, after all. In a way, form is color, for you can't have satisfying color without fine form, anything else being runny dissolution and no salute at all. The finest English cottage garden is nothing random at all but a precise composition of loose, intuitive shapes with softly definable borders. It is in these shapes that the colors fit and from these shapes that satisfaction lodges in the eye. Anything else is so much undistributed wet laundry. The standard composition of winter, birches against pines, is not effective by reason of color; it is more a black-and-white drawing than not, with a lot of the white paper showing.

But we do yearn for color in winter and the hunger for it is large, and stubbornly we continue our search. I do, but I now feel that I must go the other way. Static color is all we can achieve, and static color, indoors or out, becomes no color at all. Red goes quickly from the eye, and yellow can get quite offensive. Berried fruit, red or yellow trunks, branches of orange day after day—all of their hues have little vibration and little resonance, for winter is dry, and it is moisture that totes the ingratiations of the spectrum. Anyone who has ever tried to paint the desert comes to know this with deep frustration. In winter one has shape and sky, and shape and sky are probably all that one needs to keep the eye happy. Next year, when I see to this hill that rises just out in the far foreground of my south window, I will know what to plant. Things that produce fine sturdy stalks. Things that have large hard seed vessels and many developments of the stem. Things that sway as well—for this is the other difficulty of winter: suppleness is gone. I will have many grasses on the hill.

The hill has unredeemable problems of exposure and massive complications of soil, and rather than attempt to modify the last, I think I will plant the plants that can take such kind of brunt. Sea holly is an enormously satisfying subject for such a task. A perennial easily raised from seed, it likes its housing dry and does well in poor soil and doesn't flinch from the wind. Just as long as the sun is strong and constant, it will serve year after year without failure. When its seedheads crumble and blow, a firm clasp of claws, very like jewels gone from their settings, holds snow and ice with stunning effect. The flat-topped yarrows like lean nutrition as well and will somewhat soften the future composition. And daylilies too, for the prongs of their spent flower stalks are strong. And then there is felt-leafed mullein. Any soil will do for it, but worse is better, and its flower stalks are pure rocket trajectory made imperishable, brown bolting Jurassic shapes that birds find solid enough in the most violent wind.

There will be others, of course, in this fabric, and what I am planning, I see, will be a study in the family of brown and the way it tends to suffer a change into the most terrific of grays—rose-grays and tin grays and grays whose only quality is that they seem muffled (why one can't call such tinges *muffle*, I don't know). Warriors and sentinels will seem to occupy this little hill, spears upright and spears resting and all of them down by spring, so that I will be looking at change after all, something that would not have occurred if I had planted barberry and roses. But one element of my previous idea I will keep, and that is varieties of broom, dry and windy hills being their meat, and the family is eminently responsive to wind. I don't doubt that I will try to fuss up the picture and cushion gray and silver santolina throughout, but I hope I won't, for as charming as they are in color and shape, they are entirely too domesticated for this canvas. In a walk around the garden today in the sleet I found another, finer candidate for those gray pockets: broad-leafed sage, whose growth habit is straggle itself when not sheared or pruned, whose leaves hang tatty and soft on the coldest days and seem to unfurl a bit in direct sunlight.

And then I will mulch the whole hill in bright yellow straw, whose glitter will dull to the tone of clay itself. By that time, however, the first blue spikes of daffodils will resurrect through its indifferent cover.

Withered Things

Now begins the moment in earnest when all things withered come into their own. During the long months of winter they make a stubborn, utterly distinctive garden comprising the worn, the slow, the spent, and the broken. A just, rather admonitory group with sometimes the jerky movements of age but mostly the ability to be still, hours on end. They are enough for me. I do not subscribe to the fictitious season of "winter color" pushed forward by many writers, which at its best is but a dim recollection of what rushing sap achieves with little fuss. Wayward groupings of red and yellow twigs intended to brighten the spirit lay mine low. I am not saying that I haven't planted clumps of yellow-twigged dogwood and red-twigged dogwood (the red sometimes in front of the yellow, the yellow most often in the front of the red), for there is little pretense in them, little vibrancy, and on a bank of dried grass, above a lawn even deader, a few strokes of such mild coloring indicate elevation but little more.

What I do say is that masses of evergreens do not dupe me into thinking that their color is the hue of growth. Let us not muddy seasonal persuasions. Such greens are about as green as rotted carrot greens and old spinach in cellophane bags. Holly does not brighten my spirit. Its red fruit is quickly gone in luster. Holly fruit is grand only in September. Those others—bittersweet, inkberry, coralberry, rose hips, crabs, and even the blue-black fruits of privet—are gone in flesh and hue by the end of November and are only considered by birds in extreme stress.

Stems are another affair, and winter is their moment of glory, and it is then that I may even pick a bunch of them, whole stalks with gone blooms, for there is much light still in them and a quickness that almost seems alive. Where dry integuments have split, illumination slips through, showing fresher edges at the cut. These are the truly redoubtable, proud things that won't go down in hail or wind, stalks too tough for repeated frosts to split, stalks that go on commemorating their past and are splendid unadorned. "When I go out of life," said Colette, "I want to look like an old battle-scarred lioness, for then I will know that I have truly lived." "No makeup," said Anna Magnani on the set of *The Rose Tattoo*. "For forty-three years I have worked for these wrinkles."

Stalks take snow well and meltings too. Siberian irises with split seedpods will have a seed or two rattling in the yawning shells, and I like that low, nearly inaudible sound when the wind hisses on the path. The seeds will drop black on the snow. If they are missed by vole or mouse, the sun will be warm enough for them to melt down, where perhaps they will germinate in the spring. In the several months of unobstructed winter viewing, stalks can illustrate the success or failure of the garden. In a well-nourished patch they will be gloriously robust, and there will be pods still tight until the time of February frosts and thaws, when they will at last split, like fine books gone old in their damp, buckling bindings flaring as if one were supposed to admire the craft now that the workmanship is undone.

I think sometimes that I am seeing perennials as if for the first time, as they really are, like the old woman in *The Queen of Spades* home from the ball, headdress off, the paraphernalia of power removed one by one in a billowing pile until she stands before the audience, alone in her chamber, a tiny, bony, furious principle. Plants do not need the vanities of bees, birds, moths, odors, or ample curves. They retain, locked in their tissues and old walls, after-colors: dry, diminished tints of how they appeared in their exalted, admired states. They have taken on the far more exquisite and infinite spectrum of the withering art, which will never falter but go on fading and fading in minute, diminished steps until they enter the universe of dried fodder piled high in barns or spread over the garden as mulch. There is much in that failing.

A Mild Winter

OF ALL THE FACES of fury winter wears, the unexpected one he shows in mild winter seems craftier, crueler than the others. All things drop their guard. Cut wood before the stove stays and stays and all sorts of fine little borers and flying things hatch from little holes in the bark. The heavy coat stays on its rack and an unsuitably thin one is taken. Mice visit the untouched sack of chick-cracked corn.

Last year I was on my fifth hundred-pound sack by this time and the birds were taking a good five pounds a day. Three golden crocuses have been up and in flower, and lower branches of forsythia in the neighborhood have been cut too, and gone. Prunings of *Magnolia stellata* I poked into a thin level of cold water bloomed without the mandatory forcing bath (to their tips for twelve to twenty-four hours in very warm water), the buds remaining on the little tree losing outer husks daily. It is all very perilous to the future spring, all this movement in root and branch. Outside of an overdue cold snap, frost, quite simply, has not been through the earth—not by day or by night, and the situation is entirely springlike now, and it has been so for nearly two months, and the ocean is unusually warm. There is nothing I can do to stay the budding and the sprouting I see and the woe that is most certainly to come. Violets, of course, can take it, and those premature myrtle blooms, but not swelling fruit buds, big to such a point that they will soon lose all protective coatings. Sap is moving and so pressure is building in each stem. Only the mulberries and the oaks show no change. I take parsnip from the garden easily, but without hard frost, they are not yet truly sweet.

I am as restless as if I had spring fever and find I am more out than in but wander around with little to do. My pruning is all done. I think of moving this and that, and the more I wander through the garden, the more the whole thing seems wrong, but in this kind of mood nothing can suit. The weeping cherry outside the studio door that I have always liked and in just that spot now looks to me completely unsuited, and so too the Persian lilac by the window. Where things bloom in blue, I think of moving them and bringing in white. I have that curious feeling of disorientation that any animal asleep in its burrow will display when it is dislodged, not awake, not sleeping.

Being largely housebound in winter is something I have learned to accept and rather enjoy. A gardener's patience grows well in fine winter weather, weather of the expected brutal, forward sort. It is in the months of winter that he reviews his errors and lets them sink in. It is then that the planning goes on, then that projects are outlined, erased, and redrawn, like so many beginnings on a painting before it starts to take hold. At least I am behaving more judiciously than I used to just a year or two ago and am on guard against errors of feeling. The fine making of change in the garden must be weighed against the long hours of internal debate that take place before one acts. In odd weather—odd weather that persists—one's instincts are in sorry dress. What I might do now would be out of pique and would only have to be redone.

Whatever this winter is so far, it may well continue to be: the longest autumn on record. What I smell is late November, and what I see early April. I never thought that I would miss snow and ice, and yet I do and earnestly wish it here.

Solstice

THE SUN rose at 7:16 and set not many hours later, at 4:31, on the shortest day of the year, with window frost hard enough to tap, a day glittering and cold and solid. On the following day, however, it rose at 7:17 and set at 4:32, which gave us exactly the same dividend of light. As did the following day. Today, December 31, it rose at 7:18, into a sky wedged in seamless gray, and it will set at 4:32, which to my reckoning is definitely shorter. Something is amiss, clearly. Is the solstice out of whack, or is one of winter's nasty little trolls doing mischief in the newspapers? If so, he does it every year. It has always led me to a headache and a dark sense of having been had.

Pits

ZERO FAHRENHEIT but windless, it felt tolerable enough to make a detailed tour of the garden to see what damage had occurred, what future loss might be minimized. All—all, that is, of the visible parts, the parts above the drifts—seemed in trim. With a large broom I was able to dump mounds of snow and ice clogged in the outer forks of the cryptomerias with a small amount of the stuff falling on my shoulders; the larger measure, as usual, seemed to make it to the back of my neck. A medium-sized upright yew looked very battered, however, and I waved the branches of it back and forth to restore its shape after unloading the needles of their weight. In past years I have lost whole halves of yews, but spring and summer flushes did much to amend the damage, yews being able to sprout from their oldest sections, much like privet and almost as fast.

Where tree wrap was loosened from the trunks of autumn-planted saplings, I added some new, it being impossible to keep the twine from disappearing in the snow, so fastening the old was out of the question. Where necessary, I added whole sections of those white plastic stockings that keep rabbits from stripping the bark of trunks and branches. Given a drift around the base, any rabbit can hind up a good three to four feet, an overlooked advantage of built-up snow that has given rise to the wildest tales of a super breed. I walked out on the frozen surface of the little ponds and at last reached the wild grapevine overhanging the one next to the shed and pruned it down to livelier nubs and one long bearing arm. And so all was well, or seemed to be well. Real, permanent kills will reveal themselves in June, when large branches or whole sections of bushes will register the freeze now working cells and tissues.

After an hour, I went in and spent fully ten minutes unrolling myself from layers of wool and goosedown, foam and leather. The small choring seemed larger effort than it was, and I felt the tiring aftereffects of the snow, since its top crust couldn't quite hold me and I was continually out of balance from pulling myself free. My ideal climate would have only one week of hard winter, with a longish period of brown and wet at its beginning and following its end. With more daylight, morning and night now, winter seems to relish the opportunity of being observed.

I take a bare but sufficient protection toward it. After the annual heavy mulching, I wrap only one weeping white pine, still in its juvenile phase, in burlap, against not cold, however, but salty winds from the sea. I don't like mummies in the garden and don't grow tender specimens unsuited to the area, although the eastern end of Long Island could qualify these days for zones 4 and 5 rather than the 7 that it is in. Inexplicable Saharas as well as Siberias will visit gardens anywhere and at any time, causing horrendous losses difficult to accept, the weak with the strong, the ugly with the beautiful, and one fumbles around trying to put these visitations down to some kind of huge and reasonable sanitation, some principle of necessary selection, but there is none. Loss is loss at any rate; be it time or love, it is always awful, the heave of chaos itself. If love disappears, one has the understanding of friends, but slight is the help. For the loss of time, there may be some form of harder or more directed work in the years remaining. When a tree or a bush goes, one does have duplicates in the propagating beds, but these are, of course, small and never precisely substitute. To know that this is a condition of life is really skimpy wisdom.

The weather doesn't have me down or up, but I do sense a growing interest in what hibernation is all about. Thicker skin? More fur? Should I get a layer of fat? I do think it would be nice to finish a large Thanksgiving dinner and doze one's temperature down until April. Adequately snug in the winter studio, I am about ready to order bushes, seeds, plants, bulbs. All of enormous stamina, of course, not as if I could prevent hazard, but East End climate is so ruthlessly variable, one must automatically think of endurance. Dwarf arctic willow, then, and more, not fewer, globe thistles, and that tree mistakenly considered entirely southern, the pecan. I have seven now growing, courtesy of the Northern Nut Growers Association; whole nuts in their shell that I soaked for three days took three months to germinate, all in one large clay pot I sank last summer in the propagating bed. The pecan, even when young, has an enormous taproot, and confining them in this fashion should make them easier to unpot and line out on the east border, where Foster's field begins. Pecans have a fine, powerful shape, and I hope that the weather, during their lifetimes, will sail through their branches.*

---

* A nor'easter took them down.

FEBRUARY

❧

SOMETIMES IN FEBRUARY a state comes on me, and I am not the only gardener to be so seized. A generalized restlessness is its chief manifestation. Doors squeal open and slam shut, and sweatered only once, I go out. Many times a day.

But what is there to do? Prune the pruned? Tidy the already kempt garden? Once again rearrange tools? Sharpen them? Oil them? All the while gazing in wonderment at two witch hazels in full flush, at the French pussy willow, clouds of busy midges, swelling buds of *Magnolia denudata,* hearing the unmistakable plop of frogs, the trail of bubbled marsh gas as they skirt the muddy bottom. The very air is nutrient again, once more moist, freighted in odor. I've done ten little test digs at crucial points, and frost is entirely out of the soil, earthworms are in full race, the earth is friable and not forbiddingly chill. If this be not spring, then what season have we, or is it some hybrid come to perplex? Clouds are no longer wintry. We have had winds like those of late March. Some days grow more April by the hour.

It is hard to keep a cool head. Hard to go by the calendar and remember over and over that the average last killing frost is still the twenty-third of April, and that hoarfrost has whitened railings around the potager as late as the first week of, heaven help us, June. And out once more, this time to sprinkle a teaspoon of lime over each clematis and wait for goodly rains to wash the sweetening to the root. Two peaked-looking rhododendrons could do with a dose of Hollytone and get some. But nearly all earnest spring chores will have to wait for the outdoor faucets to be turned on. Yet the nagging goes on. Why not try some sweet-pea seeds?

Divide and transplant this or that? I am of two heads. *Zerrisenheit*, it is: "torn-to-piecesness."

I write a congratulatory note to Rosemary Verey on receiving the Victoria Medal of Honor, which will go after her OBE.

On the wall of the Madoo Conservancy, a steadily lengthening list of major undertakings for the true, the decent, may I say the honorable, open-faced, unfeigned spring. Number 31, the last, itself represents a good week's work: "prune the lower branches of the oaks." Then there is to be a drift of variegated phlox ('Norah Leigh') in the long border, dwarf goatsbeard to install in the octagon garden. The knot garden will be infilled with crushed white marble and get four fastigiate boxes from the potager, where they have grown outscale. You do see my restlessness?

And what to do with a glut of nasty onion grass? Difficult, difficult, the bulbils lying deep in the earth, the spears brittle—all must be dug up, which is a muddy, smelly chore. Oh, to squint left or right and declare them exotic little grasses, but their awfulness persists. "I am a rampant onion grass and I am a nasty little pest, survival rate unrivaled, threads of me will creep from underneath shrubs, between steppingstones. I am a swarm as intense as one of the ancient plagues of Egypt."

Number 20 is "All posts, railings, gates, benches, chairs, boxes, et cetera, anything wood, is to be scraped, repaired, painted." That's three weeks right there, with the temperature at a reliable fifty degrees Fahrenheit, else drying is impaired.

Number 8. Wisteria is invading the courtyard garden, sneaking upon and invading the *Ilex glabra,* slithering though an entangled clump of clethra, and has gone under the whole width of the summer studio (thirty feet) to emerge bright and shining on the other side.

Subsiding paths will have to be reset, the loo repainted, restocked, and I am thinking of making a rill in the center of the sunken terrace and maybe will, maybe won't, each time making a trip to see its potential in different light, which is one more opening and shutting of the door.

From a neighbor comes the sound of hammering, as buoyant and as earnest as jabs of a woodpecker.

Eden

❧

OF THE VERY LITTLE we know of Eden, clearly what has been sent down by time is not only partial but peculiarly biased—or even, if you will, censored. The memory pool of the human race functions as selectively as the individual one, however, so this is not strange. The reeking blandness of Eden would make it far too boring a candidate for reverence. I think that there must have been dramas, like storms or at the very least the coldest of sopping dews. And some withering. Else how could it have gained this transcendent power over all our dreams of place?

To be in a garden of great fertility, to have achieved the felicities of life without pain or disease or old age or death or even extreme infancy; to live without war, terrorism, or failure; to see nothing ugly, ever; to experience none of those things that cause mental, moral, spiritual, or physical dishevelment; never to be tired or lost or afraid? Definitely very wonderful indeed, but only to us today who have experienced such things in small or tall degree. But Eden ages ago was not a refuge, for the world (it *was* the world) had not yet suffered. Being cast from it would begin the woe.

Those first two knew nothing but mildness, and they were as unmarred and as soft as the vegetation. How could they have been calm, they who had always been calm? So that their Eden could hardly qualify as a luxury—or is the phenomenon of calm unending a storm in itself? Eden is a vision of happiness that is a bit thin, then, and possibly false, and we have all suffered from it. Clarice Lispector, in *Five Days in Brasilia*, writes, "We are all deformed through adapting to God's freedom. We cannot say how we might have turned out if we had been created first, and the world had been deformed afterwards to meet our needs." How seriously she felt about this is rather difficult to say, for she also, at another moment, wrote, "Just to have been born has ruined my health." But she has pertinence here.

For myself, I think that I am seriously sad about this unexamined, unexplored, lost little patch of God's creation called Paradise or Eden that we are all so nostalgic about. Its hold on us strengthens each time the world goes through pain. It is then that we compare life with that dreamy fragrant patch as if it were the sole perfection, and we seem to spend our lives in yearning—for whatever isn't here, for whatever we are not, however odd or foolish or lamentable or peculiar. And yet the relentless, unforgiving niceness of Paradise would, I am sure, drive any and all of us quite literally mad. For it to have endured so long, certain important things about it must clearly have been forgotten.

This seductive vision of Eden gets dreamed the moment each and every gardener plants, for he plants with this allurement in view. Harmony and benevolence and kindness. The root of its power is that of reciprocal behavior. We tend it in exchange for the gift of it. And yet, of all standards that a gardener might take, that of immutability is the falsest, the least acceptable. Gardens must and do change, and that is their power over us. The power of all life grows this way. All gardens must rise and dip in our expectations and give varying amounts of satisfaction. One never turns to them expecting precisely the same satisfactions.

How, then, came we to use Eden as a model, if within its confines (and we do not know whether it was walled or fenced, or whether its greenness sprang suddenly like some oasis in a patch of desert where rain recently fell) the laws of change did not pertain and all was calm and safe, a place where life never fell apart? Woe was absent, sadness unheard of. Bastion was what it was, against all of these things.

Eden was where we lived, but no garden can ever be like it. Its moments of beauty were continuous. A sweetness covered it all. Adam and Eve slept, and all the animals and the stars of the sky watched over them in a fairy tale of childhood and home. Persians and Egyptians walled their gardens to keep the dream fresh. And monks in their cloisters. And serfs their first wattled patches. And now we.

Privacy, protection, peace, spiritual pleasure, emotional joy, kinship with the earth and the songbirds and even the low, wet worm. A drawing-up from the earth and a making of green life in an ancient, alchemical gesture. On the side of nature, not against it. The desire to share it with all who come looking now and later, we hope, when we are all earth again.

Adam was my father
A tall spoiled child
A red clay tower

In Eden green and mild.
He ripped the sinful pippin
From its sanctimonious limb.
Adam was my father
And I take after him.

— Stephen Vincent Benét

Peck on the cheek and off goes the ancestor of us all, while a giraffe nibbles the boughs of fairly high growth, making much mutilation. Further, the lion in molt has left a deplorable cluster of clotted fur here and there in the grass, and Eve's first chore of the day is to groom the little meadow where this has occurred.

She sings and sighs and the sound is quite close to the well-known wails of present-day Iran where Eden has been variously placed. (The junction of two streams or rivers and, if the last, then the Tigris and the Euphrates.) Well watered as it is purported to have been, goats of last night have leaped Adam's quite pathetic attempts at fencing and have gotten at all of Eve's young lettuces, and sheep have made mischief with just about everything green and succulent except clumps of yuccas and cactus at isolated intervals, so that Eden, in many of its aspects, must have resembled today's xeric plantings.

All in all, I don't think that any of us would think very much of Eden as a garden, for it was fundamentally a sort of game or petting farm, very meadowy and meady, true, but all paths would have been trampled, flowerbeds out of the question, the little pond Adam dug for bathing taken over as a wallow by water buffalo and hippopotami and as frothed from their roiling as a cup of cappuccino. Monkeys everywhere sat in trees spitting rind and seed. Springboks made trails to the waterfall, and all were eroding.

At noon, Adam and Eve sat under a banyan tree having a banana or two, watching all of the morning's flowers go into lovely but greedy mouths.

"There go the penstemons. You might think they'd leave them alone. But no. None shall survive. All their munching has me down. This is a zoo, not a garden, and no way to live at all. Last night, the lions snoring, the hippos breaking gas, even the frogs sounded digestive. There has to be some other way, even some other life. Voles got all of my nice Abyssinian gladiolas, and you know how I love their smell. I don't, I must say, think that the Heavenly Father knew what he was doing. He's new to gardening too."

And Adam: "You know that grand and inspiring allée of poplars I planted down at the river's edge? Judging from the hoofprints and spoor, I'd bet my fig leaf on antelopes. I too am tired of seeing all my projects ruined. Pigs in the potatoes, birds taking little bites out of the tomatoes so that all rot. Raccoons in the corn. What with everything eating just about everything, I have no doubt we'll soon run out of food. Why, pray, do beavers like birch? I haven't been able to make any of that nice tea you like so much . . . Last night I had this dream about the howling wilderness outside, and frankly, it didn't seem all that bad. Empty, true, but —"

"And very, very dry, I'm sure," said Eve.

"I could dig a well, for heaven's sake, and make us a nice little hut out of wattling, and then for once we could be alone!"

"I know. All these animals. All those eyes."

"We need training in how to cope."

"Or wisdom."

"There is the Tree of Knowledge."

"But you know it is forbidden. The only thing in Eden that is."

"The other thing is a garden. At this rate we'll never have one."

"And I do, do so want one. Not grand or complicated. A nice plot of herbs. A rose arbor. When was the last time we had a decent salad? All these field greens are tough and bitter and hurt my tummy. Oh, Adam, wouldn't it be lovely to have just one utterly clean path? And a little lawn surrounded by hawthorns with a bower and a bench under it and a nice little pool I can dabble my hands in. With still water. And nothing slurping away, spoiling the reflection. They have their lives. I want ours."

And Eve began again to weep and Adam once again tried to comfort her while the animals continued their messy gambols.

The Tree of Knowledge began to look better and better.

"Isn't there strength in knowledge? What in the world could be wrong with being wise?"

"It would be nice to make a great big ditch all around us, the animals on one side and we on the other. Ha-ha! But I'd need big earthmoving equipment. And not out of wood. Something more permanent. As strong as stone. Something that could dig all by itself, if that is at all possible."

"Anything is possible, if you just know how."

"But that means knowledge."

"And knowledge is forbidden."

"But why, why, why?" And Eve's tears became more copious.

A bright red fruit glowed on the Tree of Knowledge. Out

of the forest slithered a lean green shining snake with long black glistening hair, humming a most alluring song.

Paradise relinquished, garden gained, slowly our early parents walked to the Tree of Knowledge.

The snake offered them the fruit, and thus was set their fate and the fate of each and every gardener who must toil for results.

Epilogue

IN 1994, the Madoo Conservancy, an independent charitable trust, came into being, and in the spring of that year the gardens were opened to the public on a regular schedule of Wednesday and Saturday afternoons (with tours for larger groups at other times), May through September. During my new lifetime tenancy at Madoo, I hope to continue its ramifications and enlarge its strengths. I am supremely blessed in these efforts to have a devoted board of overseers who give unstintingly of their time and thought and caring to its ongoing affairs. It is they who are entrusted with its continuity and future. It is they, when I no longer garden, who will appoint a curator in my stead. At that time the two studios and two houses will join the gardens as a study and research center.

To the memory of Elaine Benson, and to Charles Coulter, W. McDowell Hoak, Margaret Logan, Pingree Louchheim, Ngaere Macray, Marco Polo Stufano, Tina Raver, Christine Roussell, William Shank, Calista Washburn, Ira Washburn, and Jessie Wood, I give my most heartfelt thanks and gratitude for their astonishing graciousness and forbearance in the face of my impetuous and often tactless zeal. Especial thanks must go to Helen Rattray, editor and owner of the *East Hampton Star*, where these essays first appeared. Kindest thanks also to Jane Garmey, at whose urging *Notes from Madoo* reached the attention of Frances Tenenbaum.